THE POLICE OF NEW YORK CITY

THE FORGOTTEN COPS OF QUEENS

Robert L. Bryan

Dedicated to Meghan, the angel always on my shoulder.

From the Author

Thank you for downloading my book detailing the history of the police in Queens County before consolidation into the New York City Police Department in 1898.

This is the sixth book in the series about little known and obsolete police departments operating within New York City. This series is a change of pace for me as most of my previous works have been memoirs regarding my police career as well as humorous works of fiction.

You can check out all my books on my Amazon Author Page. Again, thanks, and I hope you enjoy reading about this small piece of New York City policing history. I would greatly appreciate a brief review when you have completed the book.

https://www.amazon.com/Robert-L.-Bryan/e/B01LXUSALG/ref=dp_byline_cont_ebooks_1

Table of Contents

INTRODUCTION:

I have lived in New York City most of my life. Specifically, I have lived in the Borough of Queens. Living in the Big Apple in the 20th and 21st centuries, there are certain things I take for granted. I don't think much about it, but life would suck if my garbage never got collected and my electricity seldom worked properly. Most of us, including myself, tend to take these basic sectors of infrastructure for granted, including the presence of a professional police force.

Many in the "defund the police" crowd would welcome the removal of the NYPD from New York City's infrastructure, but any rationally thinking individual realizes the important role the police play in a civilized society.

There was a time when New York City was a very different place from what it is today. It was a time when law enforcement was much different, and the Borough of Queens did not exist. When New York City came into existence, there was no professional police force that came along with it. In fact, for roughly the first 200 years of its life, New York City had no police force — at least not one we'd describe as such by contemporary standards. It had a hodge-podge of watchmen and constables, sheriffs and court officers erratically making their rounds through the streets and lanes of what we now call lower Manhattan in what was then New Amsterdam.

The first eight of these law enforcers went on duty in the mid-1600's and became known as the "Rattle Watch." Policing was primitive. There were no squad cars or walkie-talkies. A constable called for backup by shaking the rattle on his stick.

The members of the Rattle Watch also carried lanterns with tinted glass that caused them to glow green and identify them to the public at night in an era of no streetlights. When they returned to the watch house, they'd hang their green lantern on a hook outside. It's a practice that carries on symbolically in the form of glowing green sconces that flank the front doors of all 77 of the city's precinct houses, a sign that officers are inside and on duty.

The men of the Rattle Watch live on today as an obscure visual reference. The eight points on police officer's hats in the modern NYPD are a homage to the first eight members of the Rattle Watch. Their duties gradually expanded to collecting fines, recovering stolen property and banging their sticks on the table when the proceedings in a courtroom got out of hand. In reality, however, few paid any attention to them.

New York established its modern police force in 1845, in the midst of breakneck population growth, which came with rising crime and calls to fight it. City leaders modeled the department directly on London's Metropolitan Police Service, which was designed as a civilian organization, not an army. New York cops wear uniforms that are blue because London's cops wore blue — to distinguish them from Britain's military, which wore red coats.

After the Civil War, a lot of police departments and other organizations began to adopt uniforms and the rank structure. They also started carrying deadly weapons. Police departments maintained their civilian status, but they evolved into paramilitary organizations.

Corruption was endemic in the NYPD during the 19th century. It took the department until 1894 to officially call out the problem by sanctioning the first in a long line of investigative bodies. The Lexow Committee was formed to investigate corruption in the department, and they uncovered small stuff like taking free meals and taking payment for not ticketing the vehicles in front of a restaurant. Big stuff, too, like counterfeiting, extortion, election fraud and brutality were discovered.

Today, the Police Commissioner is the head of the NYPD and is appointed by the mayor. The commissioner is responsible for the day-to-day operations of the department as well as appointment of all deputy commissioners and the Chief of Department, the highest-ranking uniform member of the service.

This was not always the NYPD command structure. In 1857, Republican Party reformers in the New York State capital of Albany created a new Metropolitan police force and abolished the existing Municipal police, as part of their effort to rein in the Democratic Party-controlled New York City government. The Metropolitan Police Bill consolidated the police in New York, Brooklyn, Staten Island, and Westchester (which then included the Bronx), under a Governor of New York-appointed board of commissioners.

Unwilling to be abolished, Mayor Fernando Wood and the Municipals resisted for several months, during which time the city effectively had two police forces, the State-controlled Metropolitans, and the Municipals. The Metropolitans included 300 policemen and 7 captains who left the Municipal police but was primarily made up of raw recruits with little or no training. The Municipals were controlled directly by Wood and including 800 policemen and 15 captains who stayed. The division between the forces was ethnically determined, with immigrants largely staying with the Municipals, and those of Anglo-Dutch heritage going to the Metropolitans.

Chaos ensued and criminals had a high old time. Arrested by one force, they were rescued by the other. Rival cops tussled over possession of station houses. The climax came in mid-June when a Metropolitan police captain attempted to deliver a warrant for the mayor's arrest, only to be tossed out by a group of Municipals. Armed with a second warrant, a much larger force of Metropolitans marched against City Hall. Awaiting them were a massed body of Municipals, supplemented by a large crowd. Together, the mayor's supporters began clubbing and punching the outnumbered Metropolitans away from the seat of government. The Metropolitans gained the day after the State-controlled Seventh Regiment came to its rescue, and the warrant was served on Wood. This setback for the mayor was followed by another on July 2nd when the Court of Appeals ruled in favor of the State law. Wood knuckled under and disbanded the Municipals late in the afternoon of July 3, leaving the Metropolitans in possession of the field under the command of the four-member Board of Police Commissioners.

As the end of the 19th century drew near, it is important to note that New York City consisted almost exclusively of Manhattan. Brooklyn was a separate city with its own police force and in 1870 Long Island City established its own police force. In the county of Queens, the policing situation had not evolved much beyond Manhattan's Rattle Watch from two hundred years earlier. Many areas of Queens were rural and sparsely populated, and just like Manhattan during an earlier period, law enforcement was provided by a hodge-podge of watchmen and constables, sheriffs and court officers. All that would change on January 1st, 1898, when Brooklyn, Queens, Staten Island, and the Bronx joined Manhattan and consolidated into the Greater City of New York, with the New York City Police Department becoming responsible for policing the Borough of Queens. But let's not jump ahead of ourselves. Before we can talk about the police of Queens, we have to spend a little time talking about Queens, itself.

Green lights outside all NYPD precincts
commemorating the Rattle Watch

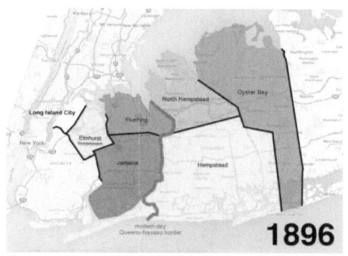

Queens County in 1896

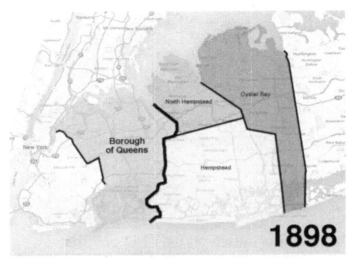

In 1898 part of Queens County became the Borough of Queens in New York City

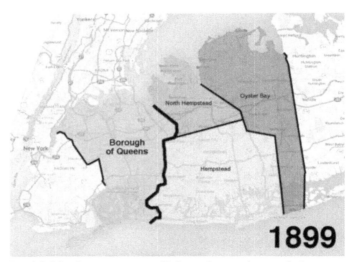

In 1899 the unconsolidated portion of Queens County became Nassau County

QUEENS:

Today, the Borough of Queens is a massive urban complex with a population of almost 1.9 million. It occupies a territory that has passed through all the epochs of the American past. The original inhabitants, the Native American Indians, gave way to the Dutch and English in the early 17th century, leaving little behind except place names and the trails that became wagon roads, some of them now major streets.

Queens County was established in 1683 as one of the original twelve counties of the Colony of New York. It was named for Catherine of Braganza, the Portuguese queen consort of England's King Charles II. At the outset, it consisted of five towns: Hempstead, Flushing, Jamaica, Newtown, and Oyster Bay.

In 1784, the northern part of Hempstead broke away, giving itself the inventive name of North Hempstead. This stemmed from a Loyalist-Patriot divide in the Revolutionary War. The northern half declared independence in 1775, while Hempstead wished to remain part of the British Empire.

The county seat was originally in Jamaica, but after the British burned the courthouse, the seat moved to the village of Mineola, in North Hempstead, close to the geographic center of the county.

During the Revolutionary War, the majority of the residents of Queens strongly favored the British. The defeat of George Washington and his forces at the Battle of Long Island in 1776 led to a seven-year occupation by British troops. Even after the American victory at Yorktown in 1781, British troops delayed their withdrawal from Queens County until they could secure the evacuation of British Loyalists to Canada who feared retribution for having collaborated with the enemy. The last British troops marched down Jamaica Avenue on November 25, 1783.

The urbanizing forces that would eventually overwhelm rural Queens began developing in the 1830s, as suburban villages were founded by individuals and realty companies for development. These forces became especially conspicuous in the 1850s. In Western Queens, land speculators bought up farms for conversion to village lots. Manufacturers, seeking rural settings within reach of New York City, scattered factories more widely at Whitestone, Woodhaven, and College Point. Meanwhile, the Rockaway beaches had begun to attract affluent summer excursionists.

The great waves of Irish and German immigration that swept into nearly all the East Coast cities during the mid-nineteenth century reached Queens as well. The Irish settled in Astoria and, to a lesser degree, in Jamaica and Flushing. Many Germans entered Queens by way of Brooklyn via Metropolitan Avenue. Middle Village, which had been English in the 1840s, became almost wholly German by 1860.

The 1890s were an era of consolidation – not only social and geographical, but political as well. The idea of a Greater New York, the merging of Manhattan, the Bronx, Staten Island, Brooklyn and Queens had been growing. In 1890, the State set up a commission to study the idea, and in 1894 the people were asked to express their opinion in a non-binding ballot. The historic vote occurred on November 6, 1894. Manhattan favored the idea. In Queens, Long Island City and the Towns of Jamaica and Newtown voted in favor. Brooklyn vetoed the proposal as did the Town of Flushing. In March 1896, the Legislature passed the Consolidation Bill, and Governor Morton signed it on May 11. All the old town governments in Queens went out of business on December 31, 1897, and on January 1, 1898, the Great City became a legal fact.

Although the population of the city expanded from about 2 million to 3.4 million, much of the new territory was still rural, and only two-fifths of all roads in the expanded city were paved. The five boroughs, which were all soon designated counties of New York State, became the basic municipal administrative units. The office of borough president was created to preserve local pride and affection.

With a land area of 109 square miles, Queens is by far the largest of the five boroughs. Had Queens County maintained its original size however, it would be almost four times bigger. All of Queens County was not included in the 1898 consolidation, as what is now known as Nassau County broke away in 1899, making the County of Queens coterminous with the one-year-old Borough of Queens. This created a strange situation during the first year after consolidation. Queens County still existed in the areas not consolidated into the Greater City, but the bulk of the county had now become the Borough of Queens and was controlled by New York City.

This confusion was solved on April 28, 1898, when the State Legislature approved the creation of a new county. It was called Nassau, taking the original name for Long Island, which honored William III of the House of Orange-Nassau. On January 1, 1899, it became the 61st county in New York State, and included Hempstead, Oyster Bay, and North Hempstead.

The establishment of Queens as a municipal borough did not create, out of the blue, a Queens identity. As already suggested, the area had many centers and diverse local traditions, and much of it still existed as farmland and open terrain. Furthermore, the new Queens County, which was made coterminous with the borough, had been severed from its former eastern territory, which had become Nassau County. The new Queens, in short, was a political artifact without a real past in the life of the people.[1]

The villages of Queens began to spring up within the towns during the 19th century. Within the town of Flushing, the Village of Flushing was incorporated in 1837, the Village of Whitestone was incorporated in 1868, and the Village of College Point was incorporated in 1880. Within the Town of Hempstead, the Village of Far Rockaway was incorporated in 1888 and the Village of Rockaway Beach was incorporated in 1897. Within the Town of Jamaica, the Village of Jamaica was incorporated in 1814, and the Village of Richmond Hill was incorporated in 1894. The Town of Newtown, which was chartered in 1665 broke away from Long Island City in 1870.

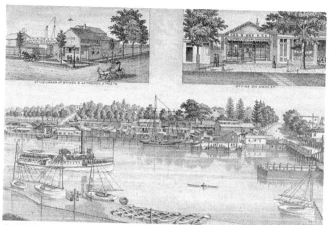

1882 depiction of Flushing

Residence of the Van Wickel family in 19th century Jamaica

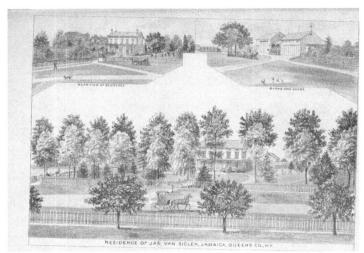

Residence of the Van Siclen family in 19th Century Jamaica

The Old Abbey Saloon in Ridgewood in 1899. The location is now Neir's Pub, the oldest pub In Queens.

QUEENS LAW ENFORCEMENT:

The history of law enforcement in Queens can be traced back to the Sheriff's Office. The New York City Sheriff's Office originated in 1626 under the Dutch. Under later English rule, the position became known as the New York County Sheriff's Office. Originally each of the city's five counties, including Queens, had its own sheriff, each of which held the widest law enforcement jurisdiction in their respective counties. Like most sheriffs in the United States, these office holders were elected to their positions. Once the city was consolidated in 1898, the New York City Police Department took over the responsibility of policing and criminal investigations throughout Queens, while the Sheriff's Office continued to focus on civil law enforcement and administering the county prison systems. Sheriffs were compensated by charging fees for enforcing civil orders in addition to keeping a monetary percentage of what their office would seize.

On January 1, 1942, the city's five county sheriff's offices were merged to become the Office of the Sheriff of the City of New York. At the same time, the sheriff's former responsibility for running prison systems was transferred to the newly established New York City Department of Correction.

Most of the Queens villages dealt with law enforcement in a similar manner. For example, the by-laws of the Village of Flushing created the office of Village Marshal:

It shall be the duty of the village marshals to exercise such powers of constables in the village conferred upon them by act of incorporation as they may lawfully exercise for the preservation of peace and good order, and for the enforcement of laws, ordinances and police regulations of

the trustees. He shall be entitled to such reasonable
compensation for special services rendered by him.[2]

On the eve of the consolidation, the New York
Police published its annual report in which it listed the
status of the various police departments in Queens during
1897.

TOWN OF FLUSHING. There was no regularly organized
police force in the Township of Flushing. The duties of
policemen were performed by constables and marshals
appointed and paid by the town.

VILLAGE OF FLUSHING. The Police Force on
December 31, 1897 consisted of 1 Captain. 1 Sergeant. 1
Roundsman. 10 Patrolmen.

VILLAGE OF WHITESTONE. The Police Force of the
village was organized on December 15, 1897, the duties of
policemen prior to that time being performed by marshals
and special officers appointed and paid by the village. The
force on December 31, 1897, consisted of 1 Captain. 3
Patrolmen.

VILLAGE OF COLLEGE POINT. The Police Force of
this village was organized July 1, 1897, the duties of
Policemen prior to that time being performed by marshals
and constables appointed and paid by the village. The
Force on December 31, 1897, consisted of 1 Captain. 1
Sergeant. 6 Patrolmen.

VILLAGE OF ARVERNE. The Police Force for the year
1897 consisted of 3 officers.

VILLAGE OF FAR ROCKAWAY. The Police Force
during January, 1897, consisted of 3 officers. And on
December 31, 1897, of 15 officers.

VILLAGE OF ROCKAWAY BEACH. This village was
incorporated July 7, 1897. Police duties were performed by
constables and special officers until October, 1897, when

men were appointed as policemen, but were paid by fees. In November a police force was organized to date from December 1, 1897, consisting of 1 Captain. 2 Sergeants. 1 Acting Sergeant. 6 Patrolmen.

TOWN OF JAMAICA. There was no regularly constituted Police Force in the Township of Jamaica. The duties of Policemen were performed by constables and marshals appointed and paid by the town.

VILLAGE OF JAMAICA. There was no regularly organized Police Force in this village. Men were from time to time employed or appointed as police constables and special officers.

VILLAGE OF RICHMOND HILL. The Police Force on January, 1897, consisted of 1 Captain. 6 Patrolmen, and on December 31, 1897, of 1 Captain. 7 Patrolmen.

TOWN OF NEWTOWN. There was no regularly constituted Police Force in the Township of Newtown, the duties of Policemen were performed by Constables and Watchmen.

PRE-CONSOLIDATION:

Today, some may think law enforcement in New York City is complicated and confusing. Even after the merger of the Transit and Housing Police Departments into the NYPD in 1995, there are still a myriad of local, state, and federal law enforcement agencies operating within the confines of New York City. Besides the men and women of the NYPD, The FBI, DEA, State Troopers, NYS Park Police, and MTA Police Officers, just to name a few, can be found working within the confines of the city.

Turn the clock back to 19th century Queens County law enforcement, prior to the 1898 consolidation and you will really see what confusion was all about. As with New York City before the birth of the NYPD in 1845, Queens was policed by a hodgepodge of watchman, constables, marshals, and special officers. There was also the Queens County Sheriff, whose Deputy Sheriffs supplemented the village police forces, and in areas like Rockway Beach, which was not incorporated until 1897, the sheriff's deputies were the only form of law enforcement. Adding to the confusion was the fact that for most of the men in Queens law enforcement at the time, their positions were not full-time occupations. Many of them held multiple positions at the same time or ran businesses along with their law enforcement duties.

We begin our journey in the village of Whitestone, because there is no better illustration of the nature of law enforcement work in the county during that era than the story of Denis Carll. But first, let's take a look at Whitestone.

According to legend, Whitestone takes its name from a large offshore rock where tides from the East River and Long Island Sound met. In other accounts the name is in honor of the White Stone Chapel, erected by townsman Samuel Leggett in 1837.

The area was, in large part, the estate of Francis Lewis, a delegate to the Continental Congress and a signer of the Declaration of Independence. The estate was the site of an English raid during the Revolutionary War. Lewis was not present, but his wife was taken prisoner and his house was burned to the ground. For a period of time Whitestone was called Clintonville after Dewitt Clinton, the former governor of New York. In the late 19th century, many wealthy New Yorkers began building mansions in the area, on what had once been farmland or woodland.

There was no one better known in Whitestone in the mid to late 19th century than Denis Carll. This man of small stature wore many hats during the many years he spent in Queens. He was a well-known figure in the Queens County Courthouse in Long Island City having served many years as a court officer and later as a United States Marshal in New York City. For years he was the police captain in Whitestone – a captain supervising only himself as he constituted the entire police force. There were at one time four special marshals, who used to get fees whenever they made an arrest, but they went out of business entirely leaving Carll as the sole member of the force.

Carll was born in Ireland in 1836, emigrated to Whitestone in 1846 and lived there for the remainder of his life. He attended the Flushing Public School. When the Village of Whitestone was incorporated in 1868, Carll was appointed janitor for the Village Hall and continued in that capacity until 1896 when a successor was appointed. He was appointed police captain when the position was created.

At some point he held the position of bailiff in the United States Court in New York City. He was elected to the office of constable for three consecutive terms and was a deputy sheriff for Queens County a number of years. He also served in the fire department.

In the first record I found of Denis Carll in a law enforcement capacity, he was working as a constable for the town of Flushing in 1870, and he was not taking a police action – he was the subject of a police action. Carll was arrested by a Whitestone Village Marshal on a misdemeanor warrant issued by a justice from Whitestone. Carll had arrested a drunken soldier and brought him before Justice Stillman of Flushing on the same evening the arrest was made. The justice wasn't feeling well and directed Carll to release the soldier in the morning after he had sobered up and to charge him enough to pay for the trouble. Consequently, Carll released the soldier in the morning and charged him a five dollar fine. Friends of the soldier accused Carll of shaking him down for five dollars. When Carll went to Justice Stillman to confirm his story, he found that Stillman had died during the night. The prosecutor of the case denied Carll had even conferred with Stillman, much less that he authorized Carll to accept five dollars before releasing the prisoner. The prosecutor further stated that the prisoner had been without food or water on the day of his arrest and clamored for a crumb of bread and a drink of water. Late in the night, his hunger and thirst had become almost unendurable, and he succeeded in attracting the attention of some boys, who climbed up to the window of the cell and gave him a drink of water from an old tea kettle.[3] Denis Carll was found guilty of extorting five dollars from William Siemers, the United States soldier. The jury recommended mercy and

Carll received no jail time. Additionally, his conviction did not hamper his further law enforcement career.[4]

In 1881, a record of Carl's testimony in a civil lawsuit again illustrated the many hats he wore. The suit was initiated by Thomas Gosling, a painter, against Vandewater Smith for a bill for work done, Denis Carll was a witness for the defense. He testified that he was a deputy sheriff of Queens, captain of police in Whitestone, town constable, janitor of a public school, and caretaker of village hall, besides being a painter by trade. "You and I worked for the same boss when we first came to this country," he said to Gosling.[5]

Another police action taken by Carll was a source of embarrassment for the Queens lawman. Before the Whitestone Village Trustees reduced the size of the police force to one man, Denis Carll, and a fellow marshal, went to a house in the village to arrest a disorderly woman. Carll went into the house not knowing the woman he wanted. He found a woman alone. As Carll entered she said, "She's in that room," and as Carll passed in she closed the door after him, locked it and made him a prisoner before departing. Carll was freed by means of a ladder. The woman was not found.

Shady politics were prevalent in New York City in the 19th century and even the rural areas of Queens were not immune from the corruption. Denis Carll, had for years maintained his office as janitor of the Whitestone Village Hall while also working as a Deputy United States Marshal of Judge Benedict's Court in New York while also performing his role as the captain of the mostly one-man village police force, He had been a strong ally of the President of the Village Trustees, Mr. Corey, and when Corey was voted out of the position the anti-Coreyites quickly moved to remove Carll from his position as janitor. Since they couldn't find any charges to base his removal upon, they settled on the scheme of declaring all offices vacant and when they refilled the office of janitor, they just happened to select someone other than Denis Carll.

Carll ran into more problems when he charged the editor of the Long Island City Tribune, Winfield Scott Overton, with assaulting him at a meeting of the Board of Village trustees. Carll said he was trying to calm a disturbance at the meeting, but Overton told him to, "Go to hell!"

Carll responded by saying to Overton, "You get out of here, you loafer." He grabbed Overton by the lapel of his coat, and they both exchanged punches before Overton was ejected.

Once again, Denis Carll became the victim of politics. When the case reached the courtroom, in a complete turnaround, Justice Kavanagh, of the Long Island City Police Court, found Carll guilty of assaulting Overton. Carll was sentenced to three days.

It may have seemed that Denis Carll was constantly playing the role of victim, but even as a one-man police force, he did have back up, albeit from an unusual source.

The Village of Whitestone was greatly excited on a summer afternoon in 1892 over an attack made by two young women on a man named Carson employed in the Central Forge Works. The day before, Carson assaulted Denis Carll, injuring him severely. The next day, Carll's two daughters both under the age of twenty, armed themselves with clubs and went to the Forge Works. They called Carson out and although he was a large powerful man and the girls small in stature, they set upon him and gave him an unmerciful beating covering his head and face with bruises. A crowd gathered and cheered the girls and after Carson ran away, accompanied them home as conquering heroes.[6]

In 1896 the Village Trustees still possessed an "anti-Carll" sentiment, and once again they set their sights on their village police captain. The trustees declared the position of police captain vacant and Denis Carll, who had held the position for over twenty years, was dismissed. This was done, they claimed, in order to cut down the expenses of the village. The little captain, however, refused to accept his dismissal and appeared in the streets in uniform as usual every day. He said the trustees had no right to oust him unless charges were preferred against him. He said he would submit his bill for services as usual and bring suit if he was not paid.[7]

At the next meeting of the Village Trustees they refused to pay Carll's bill for $40 for his January salary, on the ground that they had declared the position of police captain vacant.[8]

Carll believed the trustees could not abolish the position of police captain unless a law was enacted amending the village charter, and he insisted he was being persecuted by certain people who bore him malice.[9]

While Denis Carll was being unceremoniously dumped from the Whitestone police force, a new constable named Richard Hickman, was making a name for himself. In 1896 as a luxurious yacht lay off Whitestone, Miss Susan De Forest, the wealthy young owner of the yacht, reported that her diamonds, valued at about $8000 had been stolen from the boat. Hickman, in conjunction with Detective Fuller of New York, traced the robbery to a cabin boy, secured him as a prisoner and recovered the property. Hickman did not rest on his laurels and went right to work gathering evidence in the robbery of Mrs. M.A. Squires, of Whitestone.

Hickman arrested John O'Connor Jr., a deputy sheriff in Queens County, who was indicted by the grand jury for burglary in the second degree. This was the second time Hickman had arrested O'Connor for connection with the Squires robbery. The night the house was broken into several women who lived in the neighborhood saw two burglars leaving the house. They claimed to recognize one of the men as Thomas Brennan but did not get a good view of the other man. On this information Hickman arrested Brennan. Two days after Brennan was locked up Hickman secured a confession from him, saying that it was O'Connor who assisted him in the crime and told him that Mrs. Squires possessed valuable rugs, silverware and sealskins. Hickman arrested O'Connor who pled not guilty. At the trial his wife testified that O'Connor was drunk and asleep in bed at the time of the robbery. Mrs. O'Connor's testimony was corroborated by her 12-year- old son. Brennan was placed on the stand, and he changed his story, denying any involvement by O'Connor. The judge dismissed the charges against O'Connor.

Hickman was criticized for arresting O'Connor, only to have the judge declare him innocent. But Hickman was not satisfied and went quietly to work securing more evidence. He found more witnesses who identified O'Connor and he was indicted again.[10] Once more, however, Hickman's efforts were frustrated when several of the witnesses who were to give damaging testimony against O'Connor were not allowed to testify, including Edward Brennan, the brother of Thomas Brennan. If permitted, Brennan was going to testify that O'Connor's wife begged him to go to see his brother in jail and urge him not to squeal on her husband, and that she would swear he was home in bed drunk. Without testimony to support O'Connor's involvement he was acquitted for a second time and Constable Hickman was left frustrated.[11]

Hickman's frustration soon turned to embarrassment courtesy of his wife. The constable had purchased a new and improved pair of handcuffs, but one morning when he left for work, he forgot the cuffs, leaving them on the mantle shelf. Mrs. Hickman's curiosity led her to try on the new invention and she slipped the handcuffs over her wrists to learn how they worked. She tightened them but was amazed when she found she could not get them off. They were locked, and Mrs. Hickman worked for an hour on them before finally giving up. She could not do her housework or get the meals for her family and at night she was obliged to retire without undressing. When Mr. Hickman came home, he found his wife lying on the bed weeping and with her hands chained together. He released her and she promised never to meddle with handcuffs again.[12]

Near the end of June 1897, Richard Hickman was out of town when tragedy befell the Whitestone police force.

Henry Wendelstorf was a happy man on the afternoon of June 24, 1897. The long time Whitestone resident had been a Whitestone village marshal since 1888 as well as working as a Queens County Deputy Sheriff. His oldest daughter Annie had recently married Charles Lugar, a Long Island Railroad employee, and much to the joy of Henry and his wife, Annie and her new husband had decided to live in Whitestone.[13]

Wendelstorf was a competent lawmen who performed his duty without fanfare. Up until that fateful afternoon the most notoriety he had garnered was his arrest of Robert Merriman. The arrest was for riding his bicycle on the sidewalk, but it was significant because it was the first arrest of a cyclist ever made in the Village of Whitestone. The village had no ordinance regulating bicycles within its limits, but the arrest was made under the state law relating to vehicles.[14]

Patrick Reidy was working in a field on his farm at about 3 PM when he looked up and observed a scene that enraged him. Two men were walking across his potato patch, trampling his potatoes as they walked. Reidy began running towards the men while screaming for them to turn around and get off his property. As he drew closer to the men he had to climb over a fence, and when he landed in a clump of bushes on the other side of the fence, he was immediately pelted with a volley of rocks that struck him in the head. Reidy jumped up and ran towards the men but another volley of rocks to the head put the farmer on the ground.

When Patrick's son David heard him cry out for help. David ran toward his father's voice, and as he did, he saw two men running across the field. David found his father kneeling on the ground, badly cut and bruised. Patrick's wife assisted her husband into the house while David and his brother John took off in pursuit of the fleeing men.[15]

The Reidy boys shouted for help as they ran, and very quickly they had a crowd with them in pursuit of the two men. The men ran into a piece of woodlands, but with the growing size of the crowd after them they were soon forced out into open ground. While the chase continued someone in the crowd decided to find a policeman. The village police captain, Richard Hickman was out of town, and after some searching Marshal Henry Wendelstorf was located and led to the location of the pursuit, only to find that the two men were now holed up inside a small house with the pursuing crowd surrounding the home.

Wendelstorf directed the crowd to stay back while he approached the front door of the house. From behind the door, a man who identified himself as Thaddeus Norfleet said that if Wendelstorf did not have a warrant he was not coming out. Wendelstorf retreated out past the front gate to find that a patched up Patrick Reidy had joined the crowd. Wendelstorf directed Reidly to quickly go to Justice McKenna's home and secure a warrant. A short time later Reidy returned and placed the warrant in Wendelstorf's hand. Clutching the warrant in his right hand, Marshal Wendelstorf entered the home through the front door. A minute later he staggered out the door and fell on his back unconscious. As a group of men attempted to aid Wendelstorf the majority of the crowd rushed the home and pulled the two men out to the sidewalk. If not for the intervention of the local priest, Father O'Hara, Thaddeus Norfleet and his younger brother William Norfleet, would have been beaten to death right there. Father O'Hara had to keep the crowd calm for several hours while some of the men tried to locate another policeman. Finally, at 6 PM Marshal Rogers appeared and took custody of the brothers.[16] By that time the unconscious Wendelstorf had been removed to Flushing Hospital and the Norfleet brothers were taken to the Village Hall and placed in the jail cell. The crowd assembled outside the Village Hall, so Justice McKenna directed Marshal Rogers to take the prisoners to the jail in Flushing.

Henry Wendelstorf never regained consciousness and died the next day from the trauma of a severe blow to his head. A blood-stained broken baseball bat was found inside the home, and was determined to be the weapon Thaddeus Norfleet used to strike Wendelstorf. At his murder trial, 23-year-old Thaddeus Norfleet admitted striking Wendelstorf with the baseball bat, but he claimed he did not know he was an officer. This claim was shattered by the testimony of David Reidy. The farmer's son stated that he had been close enough to see when Wendelstorf first approached the door of the house without a warrant. He said he saw Wendelstorf display his badge to Norfleet before retreating to obtain the warrant.[17]

There was considerable outrage throughout Whitestone when District Attorney William Youngs allowed Thaddeus Norfleet to plead guilty to manslaughter and Justice Garretson sentenced him to 18-years in Sing-Sing Prison. Norfleet's younger brother, 19-year-old William was allowed to plead guilty to 3rd degree assault and was sentenced to one year in prison.[18]
There didn't seem to be much empathy for the family of lawman cut down in the line of duty. Less than six months after Henry Wendelstorf's death, County Treasurer Charles Phipps began the sale of the land owned by Wendelstorf because his wife had been unable to pay the taxes.[19]

There were some residents of Whitestone with compassion, as several men from the village started a fund to aid the family of Henry Wendelstorf. In May of 1898 Mrs. Wendelstorf was presented with $1,000. Apparently, the money was not enough or Mrs. Wendestorf did not use it wisely because her home was foreclosed on July 1, 1899. [20]

The murder of Henry Wendelstorf was the only line of duty death I could find of a pre-consolidation law enforcement officer in Queens.

Whether they had the interests of public safety in mind or they had recognized a final opportunity for political patronage, at the November 29, 1897 meeting, the Village Trustees of Whitestone believed it was in their best interest to organize a new police force that would go on duty December 15th. The force consisted of Richard T. Hickman, Captain, with a salary of $800 a year. Thomas Rodgers, Henry Steller, and Thomas Hickman, the son of the captain, were appointed policemen at $700 a year. Denis Carll was still out in the cold.[21]

On December 15th the new Whitestone police force went on duty and for the first time in its history the village was provided with a regularly appointed police force. There were two officers on night duty and one on day duty with a captain in charge. Two more appointments were still to be made.[22]

College Point originated when the Matinecock tribe sold the land, in 1645, to a group of Dutch and English settlers. One of these earlier settlers, William Lawrance became the largest land holder of the area that used to be called Tew's Neck. The decendents of William Lawrance were the only inhabitants of the land until after the American Revolution, when they had to sell a large portion of the land to Eliphalet Stratton to pay back their debts. As the Stratton's moved into the home they built on their newly acquired land in 1789, the name of the town changed from Lawrence Neck to Strattonport.

In 1838, the Reverend William Augustus Muhlenberg, rector of St. George Episcopal Church in Flushing, founded St. Paul's College on the site of what is now MacNeil Park. This institution lasted less than a decade, but its name became permanently stamped on the entire community of College Point.

In the 1850's, a German immigrant named Conrad Poppenhusen arrived in College Point and changed it forever. The process known as Vulcanization – the process of treating rubber to give it strength and durability – had recently been discovered, and Poppenhusen saw the economic potential. He was able to use hard rubber to replace whalebone (which was the standard at the time) in everything from ladies' corsets to scientific equipment. Poppenhusen built a large factory in the area, employing hundreds of immigrant workers and constructed a model community with schools, water and sewage systems, a branch of the Long Island Railroad, and a cobblestone road to Flushing. The very first free Kindergarten in the United States was established by Conrad Poppenhusen at the Poppenhusen Institute, an edifice he created for the education and enlightenment of his workers. The original core collection of what would become the library was housed within the Poppenhusen Institute.

While College Point had become known during the latter part of the 19th Century as the hard rubber capital of the Northeast, plastics would eventually take over and replace hard rubber as a component in the manufacture of small consumer goods. The rubber company Mr. Poppenhusen had established at College Point moved to New Jersey in the 1930's, and the last of the College Point rubber factories closed in the 1970's. College Point is still home to a number of small businesses and factories, and its community remains vital and involved, solidified by long-time residents and merchants, and revitalized by new immigrant families. College Point, with its many changes over time, still maintains a waterside, small-town feel.

During the 19th century, the saloons in College Point were popular spots for men from all over Queens to visit on Sunday's. Because of the volume of people visiting College Point on a Sunday the Village Trustees employed a number of marshals for the day to prevent disturbances. The marshals on duty usually had little to do because there was rarely any trouble on these Sunday gatherings. Business was especially brisk on a beautiful spring day during April in 1888. At some point in the afternoon the owner of a saloon ran out of beer, so he needed someone to go to a nearby brewery to bring back a fresh keg. Jim Clark, a big, good-natured fellow who worked as a fireman in a local factory agreed to fetch the beer. Jim retrieved the beer from the brewery, but on his way back to the saloon, the weight of the keg was tiring him out, so he stopped, put the keg on the ground and sat on it to rest for a few minutes.

While Jim was sitting on the keg, Officer Seifert, one of the marshals on duty, came along and told Jim he was under arrest for acting in a disorderly manner. Jim thought it was a joke and laughed out loud. Seifert responded by grabbing Clark by his collar to try to drag him off the keg. The officer couldn't move the large laughing man off the keg, and he became enraged. He grabbed his club, a short, thick pocket stick and began striking Clark on his head. The blows came fast and furious until the stick finally broke over Clark's head. Seifert called out to another marshal who ran to the scene and gave Seifert his stick so he could continue the beating.

Clark fought back hard, and the battle attracted hundreds of people to the spot. Finally, the two officers succeeded in dragging their prisoner to the lockup. All along the road they were greeted by jeers from the crowd. More than twenty men chipped in to pay Jim's bail and in a very short time he was out and receiving the sympathy of the enraged public. Besides the unjustified beating received by Clark, the crowd was agitated by the fact that Seifert, who was known to be very liberal in the use of his club, had moments before he encountered Clark passed a croup of New York toughs who were fighting and said nothing to them. I could find no other reference to Officer Seifert.[23]

The Board of Audit met in the Town Clerk's room in Town Hall, Flushing, and among their business was a bill submitted by Marshal Ambrose Martin of College Point, which created some discussion because it indicated that Barnum's Island was 70-miles to and from College Point. Martin's bill was for transporting Kelser, AKA "Peanuts," an emotionally disturbed man from College Point to Barnum's Island, site of the County Poorhouse, after he was charged with shooting a ten-year-old girl. The trip from College Point to Barnum's Island was actually about a 45-mile round trip, so the board was concerned that Martin's 10-cents per mile bill had been inflated. It was unclear, however, if Martin took his prisoner directly to the island or whether he stopped at the courthouse in Long Island City. I included this event because it was the only marginally negative information I could find about Ambrose Martin as I looked for some explanation of what was to happen to him.[24]

Ambrose Martin was one of the most well-known residents of College Point in the latter part of the 19th century, and not just for his contribution to law enforcement in the village. Martin was a native of Ireland who emigrated to the United States at an early age. He was for a time employed in the whalebone factory owned by Conrad Poppenhusen, in Williamsburg. When Poppenhusen established the Enterprise Rubber Works in College Point, Martin moved to the new company. He worked at the rubber company for fifty consecutive years, receiving a $250 check for his service on Christmas of 1906.

Most law enforcement jobs during that era were not full-time employment, and Martin was a village marshal in College Point and captain of the local police force for many years.[25]

Most residents of College Point were fond of Ambrose Martin. That's why the meeting held by the Village Board of Trustees on January 7, 1895, was so puzzling. The meeting included the routine business of appointing four village marshals for the usual one-year period. Many College Point residents were shocked and dismayed to learn that despite many years of service as a marshal and captain of the force, Ambrose Martin was not among the four names appointed. No reason was given for Martin's exclusion, and it was likely a case of the politics of the time. It was rumored that one of the appointed marshals was very friendly with several members of the board.[26]

The word of Martin's exclusion from the village police force resulted in a petition being circulated around the village with hundreds of signatures demanding his reinstatement being submitted to the Board of Trustees. The petition did no good.[27]

1897 was the beginning of great change for law enforcement in the towns and villages of Queens County. The Greater New York City Consolidation which would take place in 1898 would send shock waves through the policing system in Queens. In February 1897, however, the shockwaves felt by some of the police officers in Flushing and College Point were waves of embarrassment.

A phone message was received at the College Point station house after midnight on February 14th stating that a gang of robbers was on their way to College Point. The message was received by Officer Kraebel who aroused every officer in College Point before making their way to the College Point Causeway at the foot of Stratton's Hill to head off the supposed gang of thieves. The lawmen laid in wait impatiently for some time when suddenly a light wagon containing two men approached them. The police officers surrounded the wagon only to find they were the victims of a practical joke. The parties in the wagon were well known College Point men, Assessor Richard H. Williams, and Deputy Sheriff George Farrington, who seemed to enjoy the situation immensely. The two men had been drinking at Jake Hanbeil's saloon in Flushing when they decided to send the telephone message. The story of the affair spread quickly throughout the towns and villages, making the College Point Officers the subject of much ridicule.[28]

In May of 1897 the police committee of the Board of Village Trustees took under consideration the formation of a police force. Governor Black signed a bill authorizing the trustees to raise $4,000 for that purpose. At that time there were four marshals who would likely remain on the new force with four new men joining them. More than twenty applications were received.[29] In June the board appointed eight policemen to the new force, including Fred Wohlfarth as captain and Robert Williams as Sergeant.[30] At 12 o'clock on July 1, 1897 the new College Point police force went on duty. The men wore new uniforms and were the center of attention in the village. The police station was designated to be a room in Meyer's store on Second Avenue, which was equipped with cots and all the necessary paraphernalia for the policemen.[31]

Flushing was originally inhabited by the Matinecoc Indians prior to colonization and European settlement. On October 10, 1645, Flushing was established on the eastern bank of Flushing Creek under charter of the Dutch West India Company and was part of the New Netherland Colony that was governed from New Amsterdam (Lower Manhattan). The settlement was named Vlissingen, after the city of Vlissingen, which was the European base of the Dutch West India company. By 1657, the residents called the place "Vlishing." Eventually, the formal traditional English name for the Dutch town, "Flushing", would be settled upon.

Unlike all other towns in the region, the charter of Flushing allowed residents freedom of religion as practiced in Holland without the disturbance of any magistrate or ecclesiastical minister. However, in 1656, New Amsterdam Director-General Peter Stuyvesant issued an edict prohibiting the harboring of Quakers. On December 27, 1657, the inhabitants of Flushing approved a protest known as The Flushing Remonstrance. This petition contained religious arguments even mentioning freedom for "Jews, Turks, and Egyptians," but ended with a forceful declaration that any infringement of the town charter would not be tolerated. Subsequently, a farmer named John Bowne held Quaker meetings in his home and was arrested for this and deported to Holland. Eventually he persuaded the Dutch West India Company to allow Quakers and others to worship freely. As such, Flushing is claimed to be a birthplace of religious freedom in the New World. Landmarks remaining from the Dutch period in Flushing include the John Bowne House on Bowne Street and the Old Quaker Meeting House on Northern Boulevard. The Remonstrance was signed at a house on the site of the former State Armory, now the headquarters of the NYPD's Queens North Task Force and Strategic Response group 4.

In 1664, the English took control of New Amsterdam, ending Dutch control of the New Netherland colony, and renamed it the Province of New York. When Queens County was established in 1683, the "Town of Flushing" was one of the original five towns which comprised the county. Many historical references to Flushing are to this town, which included a much larger area of Queens and the area that would become Nassau County. The town was dissolved in 1898 when Queens became a borough of New York City, and the term "Flushing" today usually refers to a much smaller area.

Flushing was a seat of power in the Province of New York up to the American Revolution. During the 19th century, as New York City continued to grow in population and economic vitality, so did Flushing. Its proximity to Manhattan was critical in its transformation into a fashionable residential area. On April 15, 1837, the Village of Flushing was incorporated within the Town of Flushing. The official seal was merely the words, "Village of Flushing", surrounded by nondescript flowers. No other emblem or flag is known to have been used. The Village of Flushing included the neighborhoods of Flushing

Highlands, Bowne Park, Murray Hill, Ingleside, and Flushing Park.

In 1898, although opposed to the proposal, the Town of Flushing was consolidated into the City of New York to form part of the new Borough of Queens. All towns, villages, and cities within the new borough were dissolved. Local farmland continued to be subdivided and developed transforming Flushing into a densely populated neighborhood of New York City. A major factor in this was the Halleran Real Estate Agency. From the American Civil War to the end of the 1930s its slogan "Ask Mr. Halleran!" could be seen in ads all over Long Island, and the phrase from its maps "So This Is Flushing" became a catchphrase.

The first reference I could find to police patrols in Flushing was the establishment of night patrols in 1871. The reason given requiring the night patrols was the large number of "loafers" congregating on the corners in the evening.[32]

In 1887 the residents of Flushing were clamoring for an increase in the police force. A rash of burglaries had opened their eyes to the fact that the present force was entirely inadequate to afford proper protection to a village of nearly 10,000 inhabitants and located as it was within easy reach of the New York thieves. This clamor for police protection brought to mind the cause for the appointment of police originally. During the fall and winter of 1882 Flushing was overrun with loafers and tramps who made it unsafe for ladies and unpleasant for gentlemen to be out after dark. Crowds of young toughs gathered about the Bridge Street station and along Main Street, using vulgar language and insulting people who passed them. Fights were frequent and all efforts to put a stop to the business were unsuccessful. At about the same time the Flushing hackmen (for hire horse and buggy drivers) became famous for the outrages perpetrated upon helpless women whom they had secured as passengers. Matters reached such a state that indignation meetings were held, and the citizens went before the Board of Village Trustees and demanded to be protected. A bill was drawn up by the trustees and passed by the legislature providing that $2,000 a year should be expended for village police. The trustees appointed Charles Hance as captain of the force with two regular officers and three special officers who would be paid when requested to work.

In 1883 Captain Hance was 48-years of age. He was a native of Astoria and received his education in Astoria public schools. He learned the bricklayers and plasterers trade in Brooklyn and followed it until 1857. He then spent several years traveling around the country working in the construction trade. He returned to Brooklyn where he was married and continued in the construction trade. In 1861, he moved to Flushing and continued working on construction projects. In 1874 he was appointed deputy sheriff in Queens County where he served for many years and at one point was made Chief of Police for Rockaway Beach. In 1883 he was made the first Chief of Police for Flushing. He was also Chief of the Flushing Fire Department for six years.[33]

The newly appointed officers went on duty on Decoration Day, 1883 and found plenty of work to do. Captain Hance was determined that Flushing should have as good a reputation as any place in the country and set about to clear off the rough element. Roughs by the dozens were hurried off to the jail and penitentiary until the name of Captain Hance became a terror to criminals. The Bridge Street Kettle Gang, that had terrorized women and children, committed petty thefts, and set fire to buildings in the neighborhood, were routed in a week. The hackmen were compelled to get licenses and to stand at a respectful distance from the entrances to the depot. Ladies no longer feared to walk out at night, as they were sure that no one would molest them.

The margins between the sum of the salaries of the regular officers and the total amount appropriated left no money for the employment of the special officers. As effective as Captain Hance and his men were, as crimes began to pop up in isolated spots, it became clear in 1887 that a larger police force was needed.[34]

On December 10,1887 the Flushing Police stood watch over the meadows north of Linden Avenue, between Flushing and College Point. It was the custom of the boy toughs of those villages to gather in the wintertime on Sunday afternoons. If the weather was cold enough for skating the boys would indulge themselves on the ice for a while but ultimately, they would turn to quarrelling and fighting. The boys from the different villages would quickly take sides, and stones and sticks were used in a manner that was unpleasant for the heads of the young toughs. Sometimes Flushing won and at other times the College Point boys succeeded in driving the Flushing boys back into their own village. This little amusement had generally been confined to punching faces and throwing stones. The preceding Sunday, however, the boys had gone a bit farther as some of them were armed with pistols. When the usual afternoon fracas began shots were fired. The gunfire attracted the attention of Officer Tompkins of the Flushing Police, who charged at the boys. They were not scared off by the officer and instead stood their ground. When he told them to disperse, they jeered at him and began throwing stones. Finally, one of the boys fired two shots directly at the officer. Officer Tompkins then drew his revolver and started for the toughs who immediately ran in every direction.

It was clear to any rationally thinking person that it was impossible for three policemen to cover the entire village at once and this outrage in the meadow made it even more evident that the police force needed to be increased. Eventually, Captain Hance was able to convince the trustees to increase the number of full-time patrolmen to six.[35]

Ten years later the same officer Tompkins who had run into harm's way and the bullets of the young toughs in the meadow, found himself in another precarious situation. This time, however, it was not bullets providing the threat – it was Captain Hance. The captain claimed that he found Officer Tompkins asleep at Police headquarters at 4 AM when he should have been on duty patrolling the village. The charge upset Tompkins greatly and he vehemently denied the accusation. Public opinion was with Captain Hance as many village residents said it was about time this officer was caught, and that Hance would have found him asleep on any night he chose to visit headquarters.[36]

With consolidation into the Greater City of New York looming the village trustees suddenly decided to double the size of the village police force in the hopes that the enlarged force would seamlessly be absorbed into the new consolidated New York police department.[37]

The first name given to Jamaica was Yameco, a corruption of the word yamecah, meaning "beaver," in the language spoken by the Lenape, the Native Americans who lived in the area at the time of first European contact. The liquid "y" sound of English is spelled with a "j" in Dutch, the language of the first people to write about the area. The English retained this Dutch spelling, but, after repeated reading and speaking, "Jamaica" slowly replaced the liquid sound with the hard "j" of the English pronunciation of the name today.

Jamaica Avenue was an ancient trail for tribes from as far away as the Ohio River and the Great Lakes, coming to trade skins and furs for wampum. It was in 1655 that the first settlers paid the Native Americans with two guns, a coat, and some powder and lead, for the land which is now Jamaica.

The English took over in 1664 and made it part of the county of Yorkshire. In 1683, when the Crown divided the colony of New York into counties, Jamaica became the county seat of Queens County, one of the original counties of New York.

Colonial Jamaica had a band of 56 minutemen who played an active part in the Battle of Long Island, the outcome of which led to the occupation of the New York City area by British troops during most of the American Revolutionary War. Rufus King, a signer of the United States Constitution, relocated there in 1805. He added to a modest 18th-century farmhouse, creating the manor which stands on the site today.

By 1776, Jamaica had become a trading post for farmers and their produce. For more than a century, their horse-drawn carts plodded along Jamaica Avenue, then called King's Highway. The Jamaica Post Office opened on September 25, 1794, and was the only post office in the present-day Boroughs of Queens or Brooklyn before 1803

In 1850, Jamaica Avenue became the Brooklyn and Jamaica Plank Road, complete with toll gate. In 1866, tracks were laid for a horsecar line, and twenty years later it was electrified, the first in the state. On January 1, 1898, when Queens became part of the City of New York, Jamaica became the county seat.

In 1889 Benjamin Ashmead was a new Jamaica Constable eager for some action. He found it in an unlikely location. Not being in the business of being a "fence" for stolen property, he objected to his barn being made a receptacle for stolen goods. When Ashmead discovered George Howard storing a set of harness in his barn the constable demanded an explanation.

"Where did you get that harness?"

"A man dun gimme that harness to sell."

Ashmead took Howard into custody and his investigation revealed the harness had been stolen from the barn of William Phillips.[38]

For the next eight years Benjamin Ashmead performed admirably as a constable and at some point, he was elevated to the position of chief of the force. In June of 1897 W. J. Stanford, a trustee on the village board took it upon himself to dismiss Chief of Police Benjamin Ashmead. Ashmead was surprised to receive the note notifying him that his services were no longer needed as head of the village police department. Stanford then wrote another letter to John Hendrickson, brother of Justice Hendrickson, appointing him to the vacancy. The other board members said Stanford's actions were completely unauthorized.[39] When asked for his grounds for dismissing Ashmead, Stanford said it was because Ashmead held two or three offices and he thought two were sufficient. There might be some poor man that would like a chance.

Ashmead had made a reputation for hunting down criminals, a reputation made as town constable, not village police officer. Like many law enforcement officers of the period, Ashmead's title could cause confusion because he held more than one job at the same time. He was sometimes referred to as chief of police even though there was really no such office in Jamaica. The police force that Stanford removed Ashmead from was a Saturday and Sunday night service functioning with two men who were appointed by the trustees at a salary of $20 a month. Ashmead was still a constable and had been a Queens County court officer since 1889. He also had been performing the Saturday and Sunday night patrol duty for several years, which was the only police service under the jurisdiction of the village trustees. Additionally, a few years earlier, Ashmead organized a night patrol service that was paid for by subscription and was not connected with the village corporation. This force usually consisted of four men, but the number of men varied with the number of subscribers paying for the service. These men were invested with the power of arrest by the village authorities, and in some cases, they were deputy sheriffs. The removal of Ashmead only affected the Saturday and Sunday night village patrol force and none of his other positions.[40] Benjamin Ashmead was reinstated to the Saturday Sunday village police force after a petition with 175 names was presented to the Village Board of trustees.[41]

As the consolidation grew near, the people in the outlying areas of Jamaica began to feel anxious about the police protection in their localities and began suggesting various schemes to ensure themselves adequate protection. One of the preferred schemes required the town board to organize a town police force. If this occurred and the villages of Jamaica and Richmond Hill joined the town with similar actions, the newly formed police force of the Town of Jamaica would be in position to be incorporated into the Greater New York City police department, ensuring the town would enter the new municipality with its police force excellently organized. Afterall, the Greater New York Charter provided that all existing forces in the towns and villages must be merged into the force of the greater city. It said nothing about how long these police forces had to be in existence.[42]

The hill referred to as Richmond Hill was an accumulation of debris and rocks collected while glaciers advanced down North America. Before European colonization the land was occupied by the Rockaway Native American group, for which the Rockaways were named.

Richmond Hill's name was inspired either by a suburban town near London or by Edward Richmond, a landscape architect in the mid-19th century who designed much of the neighborhood. In 1868, Albon Platt Man, a successful Manhattan lawyer, purchased the Lefferts, Welling, and Bergen farms along with other plots amounting to 400 acres of land, and hired Richmond to lay out the community. The tract extended as far north as White Pot Road (now Kew Gardens Road) near modern Queens Boulevard. The area reminded Man of the London suburb, where his family resided. Man's sons would later found the nearby Kew Gardens neighborhood from the northern portion of the land.

Streets, schools, a church, and a railroad were built in Richmond Hill over the next decade making the area one of the earliest residential communities on Long Island. The streets were laid down to match the geography of the area. The development of the area was facilitated by the opening of two railroad stations. By 1872 a post office was established in the neighborhood, and Richmond Hill was incorporated as an independent village in 1894. In 1898, Richmond Hill joined the rest of Queens County in the consolidation into the Greater City of New York.

There wasn't much documented regarding the operations of the Richmond Hill police force other than the fact that in 1895 the force was under the command of Captain H.J. Swift, and the good captain was in a lot of trouble. The Richmond Hill Trustees were divided over the matter of charges preferred against Captain Swift by trustee James Walsh. The charges were that Swift had abused his authority, insulted two of the trustees, was a tyrant to his men, neglected his own duty, got drunk frequently and instead of watching the village generally slept in the station house or a saloon all night.

Captain Swift denied these charges and made counter charges against Walsh claiming he had secured appointments for men who owed him money and taken their wages until he was paid back and then wanted them dismissed from their jobs. Swift also alleged that Walsh, who was a Democrat, was attempting to have Swift, who was a Republican, replaced by one of his men who was a Democrat.[43]

Two members of the Board of Trustees were appointed as a committee to investigate the case against Captain Swift. On December 31, 1895, the committee released the findings of their investigation.

There were six specific charges against Swift: First, being absent and intoxicated when he should have been on duty; second, he was asleep in the station house during duty hours; third, he was present at Welden's Hotel during the progress of a ball; fourth, he committed immoral conduct during duty hours; fifth, he colluded with gambling houses; sixth, he advised officer Emdres to commit a crime.

Swift asked Officer Emdres one day if he knew where he could get carpenter's tools, such as a hammer and a screwdriver. The officer asked what he wanted them for, and Swift said they could catch some fellow drunk some night, put the tools in his clothing and then lock him up as a thief, the arrest giving the police force a good name. Officer Emdres refused to assist the captain with the dirty trick, and Swift had been harassing him ever since.

Walsh said the counter claims Swift made against him were absurd and that he actually helped get Swift put on the force. Walsh said he knew Swift may not have the right character to be a policeman, but Swift begged him and promised faithfully to keep straight. Walsh further said that he never had a man put on the force who owed him money, and never thought of replacing Swift with a Democrat friend.

Swift denied all the charges, admitting only that he might have dozed off once or twice, and claimed that he was at Welden's in performance of his duty, there being the possibility that crooks would be at the event. The last three charges were not sustained.

In the course of the investigation, the report continued, the committee noticed a woeful lack of discipline and efficiency in the police force, and they recommended that the entire force be discharged, and suitable men be obtained from outside of the village.

Finally, a motion adopting the report of the committee was carried, which was essentially a guilty verdict for Captain Swift.[44] The committee recommended Captain Swift be discharged, but a resolution was passed allowing him to resign immediately.[45]

Apparently. "immediate" had a different meaning for Captain Swift as it took another week and another directive from the Board of Trustees before Swift finally resigned.[46] On January 14th the trustees appointed Thomas S. Baldwin as Captain of the Richmond Hill Police Force.[47]

In August 1897 the village trustees voted to increase the size of the police force. The consensus of the trustees was that the current size of the force was adequate but increasing the size of the force would allow the village to enter into the Greater City of New York with greater police protection.[48]

The indigenous inhabitants of the Rockaways were the Canarsie Indians, a band of Mohegan, whose name was associated with the geography. By 1639, the Mohegan tribe sold most of the Rockaways to the Dutch West India Company. In 1664, the English defeated the Dutch colony and took over their lands in present-day New York. In 1685, the band chief, Tackapoucha, and the English governor of the province agreed to sell the Rockaways to a Captain Palmer for 31 pounds sterling.

The Rockaway Peninsula was originally designated as part of the Town of Hempstead, then a part of Queens County. Palmer and the Town of Hempstead disputed over who owned Rockaway, so in 1687 he sold the land to

Richard Cornell, an iron master from Flushing. Cornell and his family lived on a homestead on what is now Central Avenue, near the shore of the Atlantic Ocean

What is now Rockaway Beach was formerly two different hamlets - Holland and Hammels. In 1857, Michael P. Holland had purchased land and named the area after himself. Soon afterward, Louis Hammel, an immigrant from Germany, bought a tract of land just east of Holland. In 1878, he decided to give portions of his land to the New York, Woodhaven, and Rockaway Railroad in order to build a railroad station for the peninsula. The area around it became collectively known as "Hammels." On June 11, 1897, Hammels merged with Holland, and they incorporated as the Village of Rockaway Beach. One year later, it was incorporated into the City of Greater New York and became part of the newly formed borough of Queens.

In the 19th century, people traveled to the Rockaways by horse-drawn carriages or on horseback. By the 1880s, the Long Island Railroad's Rockaway Beach Branch was built to serve the Far Rockaway station. Far Rockaway incorporated as a village on September 19 of 1888.

Remington Vernam and the Ocean Front Improvement Company began developing an area on the peninsula. The name, Arverne, was suggested by Vernam's wife, who derived the name from the legible part of his signature, "R. Vern."

By 1898, the area was incorporated into the Greater City of New York, which included Far Rockaway, Rockaway Beach, and Arverne.

On August 5th, 1896 the trustees of the village of Arverne by the Sea, adopted a resolution appointing

George Hemmert police constable, without regular compensation, his term to continue during the pleasure of the board. On December 1, 1897, the trustees of the village adopted a series of resolutions appointing five men, including Hemmert, to the newly established Arverne police force. Fixed salaries were set for all the new policemen except Hemmert. Hemmert alleged that compensation had been fixed for him by providing that he should be paid fees for his services, an allegation the village board did not deny. Subsequently, the only payment made to Hemmert from village funds was for the sum of $4.00. No provision was made for paying him anything in the village tax budget for the fiscal year of July 1, 1897 to June 30, 1898, and it was evident that Hemmert was to receive fees for his services as would be payable to a constable for like services.

Far Rockaway had such a small police force, it was difficult to properly address issues of crime when they developed. In 1887, Captain John C. Walsh was roundly criticized for his response to a series of robberies and assaults. Walsh explained that the two worst cases occurred out of the sight of any patrolling officers. It was bad enough to excuse the crimes because they were committed on a back street, but in reality, the robberies were committed on Cornagua Avenue, one of the main roads in Far Rockaway. The captain had no response to the fact that a newspaper reporter had determined the identity of the gang responsible for many of the crimes in a few hours while the police had no leads after many days.[49]

On the evening of December 2, 1897, the newly appointed police force of the Village of Far Rockaway went on duty for the first time. The force consisted of

53

Chief John C. Walsh and eight patrolmen. Additionally, there were three special officers on night duty and seasonal duty.[50]

In Rockaway Beach in 1888, there was an incident that was not considered a line of duty death, but it was no less tragic. A terrible accident, resulting in the mangling almost beyond recognition of a faithful and efficient member of the Rockaway Beach police force occurred at the beach. The victim was Officer Kane. He had been performing his arduous duty during the terrible heat in assisting to keep the hot and perspiring army of pleasure seekers in order, and shortly after 9 o'clock he started for Hammell's Station, where he took the train home.

The train left at 9:45 and was filled from end to end with people going to Brooklyn and New York from the beach. When Officer Kane arrived the heavily laden train was just leaving the depot. The unfortunate man thought he saw a chance to board, and disregarding the cries of warning to him, he grasped one of the handrails of the fourth car and tried to swing himself aboard. But he miscalculated the distance, his foot missed the steps, his hands slipped from the handrails, and he fell onto the tracks with several of the heavy steel cars passing over his body killing him at once.

Officer Kane had been on the police force at Rockaway Beach for many years and was known as a most efficient officer.[51]

In Long Island City, Mayor Gleason was famous for looking the other way while illegal gambling houses operated, as long as he profited. But when he received enough public and political pressure he acted swiftly and decisively. Such was the case in 1889 when the mayor issued orders to his police force to raid a newly opened pool room in Blissville, not far from the Calvary Cemetery. It was the same place raided by the police a year earlier, when the proprietor, Michael Kearney, a notorious cock fighter, was arrested and later indicted. Preparations for opening the pool room were underway for the two weeks and all the time Mayor Gleason had a detective on the inside. Business was opened with a boom, but it was not for long, as police were in waiting to pay their respects to the gamblers and the manner in which the raid was planned and executed could not have been surpassed. One hundred and fifteen men were hemmed in and arrested, including Michael Kearney. Everything in the nature of gambling paraphernalia in the building was seized by the police. The big surprise of the day was that Owen Kavanagh, the captain of the Rockaway Beach police was arrested in the raid. At 8:00 PM Mayor Gleason, who was also a magistrate, opened court and the prisoners were paraded before him. Captain Kavanagh was discharged.[52]

Rockaway Beach was not a high crime area, but it experienced many different types of crimes, including police impersonation. George Hallock, 27, and William Gardner, 24, were arrested by Sergeant Bergenheim and Officer Monahan of the Rockaway Beach Police on the complaint of William Mahoney, who charged them with impersonating police officers. Mahoney and a friend went to Rockaway Beach on Sunday and missed the last homebound train to Brooklyn. The hotels were so crowded the two men could not find a room, so they passed the time by walking the beach. At 4 AM they became tired and sat on the veranda of William Adams' Hotel on Seaside Avenue. While they were resting, Hallock and Gardner approached and placed them under arrest. Mahoney and his friend were led in the direction of an unknown destination when they came upon Officer Monahan and Sergeant Bergenheim. Not realizing that Hallock and Gardner were police impersonators, Mahoney declared to the real cops that they were being arrested for no reason. The real officers immediately placed Hallock and Gardner under arrest for impersonation.[53]

Sheriff Norton, of Queens County appointed Deputy Sheriff W.H. Allen of Flushing, captain of the police force at Rockaway Beach for the season in 1893.[54] Captain Allen was highly regarded, but in 1894, a citizens committee led by Dr. George A. Brandreth levied charges of corruption against the force, and in particular Captain Allen and his men for extorting money from hotel keepers and residents before providing them protection; permitting gambling halls to operate; and sergeant Stanton and Policeman John Walsh were accused of drinking with disreputable women. A hearing into the charges was held at the town hall. The principal witness was an ex-policeman named Shappart, whose testimony was impeached when Captain Allen pointed out that Shappart had been discharged as a policeman for taking money from a brothel. The tribunal consisted only of Sheriff Norton, the man who appointed Captain Allen. Not surprisingly, the charges were deemed to be unsubstantiated, and the hearing ended in time for everyone to attend a dance being held in Captain Allen's honor.[55]

The politics of Rockaway Beach were as important and influential as in New York City. Since the Queens County Sheriff controlled the Rockaway Beach police force, when Sheriff Norton was defeated in the November election by Sheriff elect Doht, it signaled the end for Captain Allen, as Doht was sure to appoint his own man as captain of the force. The Rockaway Beach captain's position was a particularly political office. One experienced deputy sheriff expressed how undesirable a job it was, explaining that the captain of the Rockaway police was constantly harassed by politicians, and that the harassment combined with the fact that nine-tenths of the policemen were appointed through the influence of political leaders prevented the captain from controlling his men.[56]

Eventually, Sheriff Doht appointed William Methven as captain of the Rockaway Beach police. Methven was born in Scotland in 1851 and came to the United States in 1875, settling in Newtown. Five years later he moved to Flushing as an employee of H.C. Howells. A few years later he opened a hotel in Flushing and then purchased the Flushing Stables. In an example of how many law enforcement officers in the 19th century held multiple positions, Methven was appointed a Deputy Sheriff in Queens County. Even as a law enforcement officer Methven performed multiple roles, creating titles that could be very confusing. For example, even though Methven was leading the Rockaway Beach force, in June of 1896 he was present in Long Island City serving a letter on behalf of Sheriff Doht on the manager of the Eureka Athletic Club. The letter warned the establishment that the Sheriff was aware of a scheduled prizefight at the site, and that such an event would result in the arrest and prosecution of all principals involved. Once this duty was done Methven was back to Rockaway Beach to resume his role as captain of the force.[57] A reception for Captain Methven was held in Murray's Grand Ocean Pavilion which was attended by nearly a thousand people.[58]

As consolidation drew near, Rockaway Beach, like the other towns and villages of Queens, authorized an appropriation of $8,000 for the maintenance of a police force.[59] The proposition was carried by a vote of 76 to 45. The force as appointed by the trustees would consist of a captain, two sergeants and eight patrolmen. With the new police department also came a new captain. William Methven was out, and he returned to focusing only on his duties as a Queens County Deputy Sheriff. The newly appointed Captain was Louis Kreuscher, a 32-year-old long time resident of Rockaway Beach. In another testament to the politics of the day, Kreuscher was a trustee of the village, but he resigned to accept the position of police captain.[60]

The village of Newtown was founded in 1652 by English Puritans from Connecticut and Massachusetts. The village was located approximately 7 miles from the growing city of New Amsterdam and just east of the settlement at Maspat (now called Maspeth), which had been abandoned following threats and attacks by local Lenape Native Americans. When the British took over New Netherland in 1664, they renamed the village Nieuwe Stad (New Town) to maintain a connection to its Dutch heritage. This was eventually simplified to Newtown. In a deed dated July 9, 1666, the settlers took title to the lands of Newtown from the Native American tribes.

Residential development in the area was spurred in the 19th century by the completion of a horsecar line, the Grand Street Line, which reached Newtown in 1854. The Long Island Railroad's Main Line was built through Newtown in 1876, attracting more residents to the neighborhood.

Cord Meyer bought land at Broadway and Whitney Avenue in 1896, and proposed that the town be renamed "Elmhurst", meaning "a grove of elms." In 1897, one year before Queens County was incorporated in the Greater City of New York, the town was renamed. The renaming was done partially to disassociate the town from nearby Maspeth and the smelly, polluted Newtown Creek, and partially to celebrate the elm trees that abounded in the area.

Most of Newtown's police problems generated from the festivals and gatherings at several picnic grounds in the town. The good times experienced by most participants also attracted scam artists and hooligans requiring police intervention. For example, there was an 1889 festival at a Newtown picnic ground held for various labor organizations and their families. Around 10 PM the good-natured tenor of the crowd was broken by the action of a crowd of men who were not members of any particular organization. One of the rules made by the organizers of the festival was that when a participant in the festival left the picnic grounds, they could not return without presenting a ticket or paying the 25-cent price of admission. In other words, no return tickets were given. This rule caused a dispute which resulted in punches being thrown and serious injuries. Bernard Degnan, the well-known labor leader stood at the gate and notified all who left the grounds that they could not return without paying again. Alongside of him stood a big special officer belonging to Queens County. A group from the laborer's union heard Degnan's warning but departed the festival anyway. A short time later these same laborers returned and demanded to be admitted without additional payment. Degnan refused to allow them access and directed the special officer to move the group away from the entry gate. As the policeman moved towards the group, a burly laborer punched the officer in the face, and in an instant, there were seven or eight men striking at the officer with sticks and clubs. The policeman was knocked down and received a deep cut on his forehead. Despite his injuries, the officer regained his feet and struck his first assailant on the head with his club. At that point nothing short of a riot broke out with the laborers and their allies fighting the organizers of the festival and their friends. Several men drew revolvers and many women screamed and ran inside the ticket takers house. The laborers forced their way into the picnic grounds and ran into the crowd. Five policemen, with Mr. Degnan leading them, ran through the park looking for the original troublemakers. All the laborers who started the trouble were captured. The burly man who had thrown the first punch, his face covered with blood, was taken to the Newtown police station, while all the others were simply told to go home.[61]

In 1896 police from all over Queens and Brooklyn had to be called to the picnic park in Maspeth when fifty-nine Russian soldiers were part of a riot at a picnic gathering. The large number of soldiers was problematic enough, but each soldier brandished a long saber which caused additional havoc in the park.

The riot occurred at a picnic given by the Independent Order of Russians, to which Russian Hussars had been invited. Both were military organizations and the men all carried mammoth sabers. A fight was precipitated when Queens Deputy Sheriff Washington Sherry clubbed the president of one of the organizations for arguing with him while he was making an arrest. The friends of the clubbed man came to his rescue and a general melee followed. During the police response to the riot, Deputy Sheriff Frank Bowman was stabbed with a saber.

Eventually, all the soldiers and their sabers were transported to Newtown police court where they were arraigned on rioting charges. The initial prognosis for Deputy Sheriff Bowman was that he would not live, but I could find no further record of his condition.[62]

Aside from the problems with social gatherings, Newtown was not a powder keg of criminal activity. Every now and then, however, crime did rear its ugly head. In 1893 Constable George Hooks of the Newtown Police Force arrested Hugo Schmidt and Frederick Eberhardt on a charge of stealing a cow worth $150, from the stable of John Schneider, the foreman of St. John's Cemetery in Middle Village. The men took the cow to a barn where they killed it and were in the process of dressing the carcass to sell in Brooklyn when the constable discovered them. Eberhardt grabbed an ax and attempted to strike the officer with it. Hooks defended himself with his club and had to beat the crook into a state of near unconsciousness before he submitted.[63]

Constable Hooks law enforcement activities were not limited to crimes against animals. A few weeks before the cow theft, Hooks was involved in a serious case involving a young girl.

Frederick Zieg and Frank Martin were two German farm hands who had been working around East Williamsburg and Middle Village. They were both thirty years old and had developed reputations as troublemakers in the saloons in the Middle Village area. On a Sunday afternoon the two men were walking along Metropolitan Avenue with Zieg possessing an ax and Martin holding a club. When they passed the home of John Tumar, they saw Mr. Tumar's 16-year-old daughter Rieka, sitting on the front stoop. No one else seemed to be around, so the two men entered the front yard and approached the girl. Zieg asked her to kiss him. The girl attempted to run into the house, but the two men seized her and threw her to the ground. The girl resisted and screamed loudly for help. One of the men choked her to stop her cries, but her parents had already heard her pleas for help. When the men saw the parents rushing toward them, they released the girl and turned their attention to the parents. Zieg picked up his ax and struck the mother on the head, cutting a frightful gash, while Martin gave the father a terrible beating with his club. By this time, neighbors had become aware of the incident and rushed to aid the family. The two men fled, but because of their reputation as violent thugs, no one chanced to pursue them.

A warrant for the arrest of the two men was issued and given to Constable Hooks. Hooks found the men in a hut in the Jamaica Woods the next morning. They initially resisted the constable, but when he drew his revolver, they submitted to arrest and were taken to the Newtown jail.[64]

ROCKAWAY BEACH POLICE FORCE.

LOUIS KREUSCHER,

Captain of Rockaway Beach Police
At time of Consolidation

Captain Charles Hance

CAPT. RICHARD T. HICKMAN.

THE NYPD ARRIVES IN QUEENS:

With the imminent arrival of the Greater City of New York, and with it the consolidation of all the police departments into one New York City Police Department, the fate of the Queens policemen would be in the hands of a new administration in a new city. In the politically charged environment of the era, the framers of the new City Charter were careful to include language in the document to insure one political party could not seize control of the consolidated police force for its own purposes. As a result, Greater New York's first elected mayor, Robert Van Wyck, a Democrat, was required by law to appoint a bi-partisan police board to oversee the department. The board consisted of four commissioners, two Democrats and two Republicans. One of the appointees, Democrat Bernard York was appointed President of the Board.

There was controversy almost immediately because the Charter mandated that the first chief of police had to be either the New York City Chief of Police or his deputy, or the City of Brooklyn Chief of Police or his deputy. None of these four candidates suited Richard Croker, known as Boss Croker, the head of the Democratic political machine in Tammany Hall at the time. Croker wanted his benefactor, Mayor Van Wyck to appoint Tammany favorite William "Big Bill" Devery. But Devery was a mere police captain, which made him ineligible for the position. Maneuvering Devery into position would take some time. In the interim, the board named John McCullagh Chief of Police.

On January 1, 1898, McCullagh issued the first order of the new Police Department of the City of Greater New York.

Police Department of the City of New York
300 Mulberry Street
Office of the Chief of Police
New York, January 1, 1898
General Order No. 1:
Sir – It becomes my duty to announce to the officers and members of the police force of the City of New York that the Board of Police of the Police Department of the City of New York was this day duly organized, the following commissioners were present, namely: Bernard J. York, Thomas L. Hamilton, John B. Sexton, William E. Phillips. Commissioner Bernard J. York was elected president and Commissioner Thomas L. Hamilton was elected treasurer of the board.
At a meeting of said board held on this day it was resolved that the present chief of police of New York City, John McCullagh, be designated the acting chief of police until further action of the board.
Also, resolved that the present superintendent of police of Brooklyn, John Mackellar be designated as acting deputy chief of police of the Borough of Brooklyn until further action of the board.[65]

In retrospect, that the consolidation would be problematic for the local police departments in Queens should have been obvious. Politicians and police administrators from New York City did not think very highly of the lawmen in the outlying county. For example, in January 1898, Mayor Van Wyck attempted to shoot down Police Commissioner York's request for additional policemen in the Borough of Queens by arguing that "One New York policeman is equal to four country constables."[66]

Another unforeseen consequence for the local policemen of Queens was the animosity between Brooklyn and New York City. The City of Brooklyn Police Department considered itself equal, if not superior to the New York City Police, and they resented having to bend to the will of their neighbors across the river. Sarcastic remarks flew out of Brooklyn noting that there had been no scandals among Brooklyn's captains and that no huge fortunes had been made by the men in command of the Brooklyn Precincts. The Brooklyn department even balked at having to transition to the forms being used by the New York City Police.

How did this effect Queens? Everything regarding the consolidation of the City of Greater New York was new, including a new mayor and a new board of police commissioners. The new administration could not give a legally binding order until January 1st, and Brooklyn did not intend to comply with any orders until that time. Therefore, the fate of the Queens police departments could not even be considered until after the new year.[67]

The Board of Police Commissioners had serious reservations regarding the town and village police forces in Queens. They considered the manner in which the villages had organized police forces or increased the size of existing forces in the waning months of 1897 as tantamount to fraud and a blatant attempt to load the new Greater New York Police Department with scores of political patronage jobs for cops appointed just before the consolidation.

In an attempt to straighten out the situation as quickly as possible, the Board of Police Commissioners passed the following resolution on January 2nd:

Resolved, That the acting chief be and is directed to assign such a number of inspectors or other officers as he may deem necessary for the purpose of making a thorough investigation as to the status of persons claiming to be members of the police department in the Borough of Queens, and that they also investigate and report as to the condition of property belonging or claiming to belong to the Police Department in said Borough.
That the acting chief be directed to assign such officers and men as he may deem necessary for the purpose of policing such Borough.

High ranking members of the New York City Police Department would be immediately dispatched to the villages of Queens to access whether the men of these departments were really policemen or political hacks appointed because of their patronage as the consolidation clock struck midnight.[68]

The greatest consolidation excitement was generated in Queens when Police Captain Anderson and Sergeant Elderbrandt from police headquarters in New York visited Flushing just before the new year and inspected the Town Hall with a view of ascertaining its desirability for a police station under the Greater New York Police Department. The officers expressed themselves as satisfied with the building and its location and stated that if it was decided to use it for the purpose mentioned more cells would be constructed on the lower floor, while the opera house would be used for a drill room.

The news that the Police Board of New York City had taken action to extend the police service under the Greater New York without delay in the outlying districts created a ripple of excitement in Flushing, College Point, and Whitestone, where new forces had been appointed. It was rumored that the Police Board had not looked favorably on the actions of the trustees of these villages, who had been appointing policemen right and left in the hope that they would walk right into pay, privilege and the pension fund of the greater city. All the policemen appointed in such a hurry, it was feared, would cease to exist officially on New Year's morning, as their term of office lapsed with that of the village trustees who made them. All the village policemen Queens waited anxiously for word from Mulberry Street Police Headquarters in Manhattan.[69]

The new year turned out to be anticlimactic. Queens was now a Borough in the Greater City of New York, but nothing seemed to change for the policemen of the Borough. On January 2nd, however, the New York City Police Department began to show itself in Queens.

A number of experienced detectives swooped down upon the three incorporated villages of Flushing, College Point and Whitestone. The news that these officers had arrived in the villages created considerable comment among the residents. The members of the different forces were anxious and still on duty, determined not to surrender unless forced to do so.[70]

Meanwhile, Denis Carll created considerable gossip by the announcement that he still considered himself to be captain of the Whitestone police. When the new year arrived, he reported to New York for duty and was ready to receive orders from the department.

When the Whitestone Village Trustees appointed a new police force and captain on December 15th, Carll contended that if the trustees could not appoint a police force in 1892, they could not do so in 1897. Carll sent a letter to the police board stating that he was still the legally appointed captain of the village and in his closing remarks said, "I most respectfully report to your honorable body for duty and shall at all times hold myself in readiness to obey your order."[71]

Carll made the situation for the newly appointed captain of the Whitestone Village police force, Richard Hickman, very uncomfortable. Like all the other policemen in Whitestone and the other villages in Queens, Hickman waited anxiously to see if he would receive a position in the New York City Police Department. His anxiety was compounded by Denis Carll. Carll was now working as a truant officer for the Board of Education, but he was still very vocal in and around Whitestone in his claim that he was still the rightful captain of the Whitestone police force.[72]

Richard Hickman was born in Baltimore in 1847. He served in the Civil War in the 210th Pennsylvania Volunteers and was wounded in the left leg. He was honorably discharged from the army at the close of the war. In 1871 he moved east, and soon afterward went to Whitestone to reside. For many years he was a road building contractor, and in 1878 was appointed constable in the town of Flushing. He served later as a deputy sheriff and was also the proprietor of the International Hotel in Whitestone. In 1897 he was appointed captain of the Whitestone police force and held the office until the advent of Greater New York.

Inspector George Rhodes was appointed by Chief McCullagh to investigate the police departments of Queens. He first made a tour of Flushing on January 4th, visiting the Town Hall and examining the cells and court room. He was well satisfied with the police force but was non-committal regarding the outcome of the old police.

He told them to continue doing a good job, and that the Board of Police Commissioners was absolutely impartial and that he was sure the people of Flushing would be happier than they had ever been regarding policing matters.[73]

On January 6th, Inspector Rhodes was all smiles when he arrived in Richmond Hill to examine the police operations. Richmond Hill had not experienced significant changes with the new year. The village police force still patrolled the village. A contingent of policemen from Manhattan had been sent to the village, but there had been no action taken to indicate that the old village force was being absorbed into the new city department. In fact, the new arrivals from Manhattan seemed to be acting as if there were no police in Richmond Hill. Sergeant Weiser, who had set up his headquarters in Jamaica said he was not sure what would be done at Richmond Hill.[74]

After a careful examination of the records and personnel of the force, Inspector Rhodes pronounced himself highly pleased and declared Richmond Hill the best organized force in the borough. He told Captain Baldwin to keep his men at work until further notice.[75]

Inspector Rhodes' good will tour continued the following day at Rockaway Beach. Hopes were high when the Inspector seemed to be pleased with the condition and operations of the police. [76]

A month past and the policemen in Queens still did not know their fate. They continued to perform their regular duty while anxiously awaiting some instructions from the city that would indicate they would be absorbed into the large department – but no word came.[77]

On February 1, 1898, the police from Manhattan and Brooklyn came to Queens. The did not come like

Inspector Rhodes, with the hand of friendship. This time they crossed the river as nothing less than an invading army.

Chief McCullagh detailed a number of officers from Manhattan and Brooklyn to police the Borough of Queens under a resolution of the board on February 1st. The board resolved to direct the chief to make arrangements for policing Queens and the chief assigned six sergeants, twelve roundsmen, and 72-patrolmen to perform duty in Flushing, Newtown, College Point, Jamaica, Richmond Hill, Rockaway Beach, Far Rockaway, and Whitestone.

Deputy Chief Elias Clayton was assigned to establish and take charge of the police at Richmond Hill and Jamaica. Inspector Brooks would command Newtown and Flushing, while Inspector Rhodes took command at College Point and Whitestone, and Inspector Cross did the same at Far Rockaway and Rockaway Beach.

The officers and men met in Brooklyn and started for their various stations during the morning. The officers received orders from the chief not to recognize any of the attempted hold-over police in Queens who were appointed before consolidation.[78]

As the men assembled at their directed locations, they looked like lost boys trying to figure out where they were supposed to go. They claimed they knew nothing about their destination. At 11:30 AM the men bound for Richmond Hill and Jamaica were addressed by Inspector Clayton, who for the first time told the men where they were being assigned. One section of this group comprised of a sergeant, two roundsmen, and ten patrolmen were dispatched to Jamaica, where they were to establish headquarters in the old town hall. The second group under Inspector Clayton, consisting of a sergeant two roundsmen and nine patrolmen were sent to Richmond Hill, about two miles west of Jamaica, and were instructed to take possession of the Town Hall from the old force of constables.[79]

The members of the police force of Richmond Hill were disappointed over their failure to become members of the greater New York force. The men in the village felt certain that they would stay and everybody who had studied the charter at all assured them that if any force outside of Brooklyn would be transferred to the police department of the greater city, it would be Richmond Hill.

Suddenly, without warning came the notice that the old force would not become part of the greater city police, and along with the notice came a sergeant and ten patrolmen. Many residents of the village felt that a wrong had been done to the men, and the men vowed to fight the issue in court.[80]

The dismissed village policemen were not the only upset officers. Many of the invaders from Manhattan and Brooklyn were highly upset over the arbitrary manner in which they were transferred, especially to Richmond Hill, which they very quickly christened the "Klondike Precinct." Sergeant White, who had previously been assigned to the Central Office Squad in Manhattan, suddenly found himself in command of a squad of cops in the wilderness of Richmond Hill. When Sergeant White took possession of the town hall from Captain Baldwin of the village police force, he said goodbye to Baldwin and wished him well. His final words to the deposed captain were, "I expect I will be a full-fledged hayseeder inside of six months."[81]

A force of 33 policemen from New York City swooped down upon Flushing late in the morning on

February 2nd. The men were under the command of Sergeant Contrell and Inspector Brooks. The men were distributed throughout the town as follows – Flushing 13 men – College Point 10 men – Whitestone 10 men. Although the local policemen were expecting some changes, they were still taken by surprise by the arrival of the New York force.

When the New York police arrived, they took possession of Flushing Town Hall, and the Flushing Village Police were informed by Sergeant Contrell that they were relieved from duty. Captain Hance was directed to instruct his men to remove their uniforms immediately.

Even though the village police force had been doubled in size in the days just prior to consolidation, the Flushing police force was different than many of the other village forces in Queens in that it had existed for twelve years under the command of Captain Hance. Additionally, before passing out of existence, the village trustees made provisions for the maintenance of the police force by appropriating $4,700 to pay the salaries of the policemen for a year.

The arriving New York City policemen, who were total strangers in the town, were immediately assigned to duty. The local policemen, who had only recently spent $50 to purchase new uniforms, said they planned to fight their dismissals in court.[82]

In Whitestone, Inspector Rhodes sought out Captain Hickman and like the general of a conquering army he asked if he would surrender to the New York police authorities without any resistance. He explained to Hickman that in the event of his refusing to do so he would be liable to arrest for usurping the functions of a police officer. Captain Hickman said he was willing to surrender, but he would do so under protest, and with that statement, his functions as a police officer ceased. The captain immediately retained a lawyer to bring a lawsuit for his reinstatement.

While this controversy swirled, Hickman suffered a personal tragedy. Charles, his 21-year-old son, died. The young man had undergone an operation for appendicitis a year earlier, and when complications developed, he had to be operated on a second time. An abscess that had formed in the abdominal cavity was removed, but blood poisoning set in that proved fatal.[83]

The arrival of Inspector Cross and Sergeant Westervelt along with a squad of New York City policemen in a special train resulted in weeping, wailing and gnashing of teeth by the members of the old police force of Far Rockaway. The local force had hoped vainly that they might be recognized, but the last glimmering ray of hope was ruthlessly dispelled when Inspector Cross with his subordinates in full uniform, went direct to Village Hall and assumed control of affairs. The Inspector read an order signed by Chief McCullagh, in which the inspector was directed to proceed to Far Rockaway forthwith to organize a division of the Police Department of New York City. John C. Walsh, who had been appointed chief by the former trustees of the village, entered a protest, but was ordered to take off his uniform by Sergeant Westervelt.

Not a solitary member of the local force was to be included in the new force, and there were long faces and bitter protests, especially among the old force who believed that under the Charter they could not be removed. They declared they would bring the issue up later in court. Inspector Cross also read to the old force the section of the statutes under the penal law where it was shown that any person impersonating an officer by wearing the regulation uniform was guilty of a penal offense. This was duly explained, and the old force stripped off their uniforms.

Sergeant Westervelt was placed in command of the new precinct and detailed his force to cover the village. The next day the old force went to the village hall but were given no recognition by the sergeant. The members of the old force declared they would report for duty every day until the courts pass upon their right of recognition or deny their legal standing.[84]

At Rockaway Beach, Captain Kreuscher had been in command of the police force since September. Prior to his appointment Kreuscher had been engaged in the oil, crockery, and glassware business. Apparently, what qualified him for the position of police chief was his prominence in political and social circles as well as the fact that he was a trustee of the village. At 3:30 PM on February 3rd, Kreuscher and his force were taken by complete surprise when Inspector Cross and thirteen New York policemen appeared at their Seaside Avenue police station and took immediate control of police operations. Inspector Cross explained to Captain Kreuscher that he had been sent by the chief of police of the greater city to relieve him of his command. He asked Kreuscher to call in all his men, and then, going to each one separately, told them of their discharge from further duty. The station house was placed under the command of New York City Sergeant Townsend. The news of the appearance of the police from New York City created consternation among the villagers, and large crowds gathered in front of the police station, several officers being required to disperse them. Captain Kruescher was instructed to order his men to remove their uniforms.

Captain Edward Stroschein and his policemen at Arverne were also called into their station house and relieved from duty. All of the men claimed to have been legally appointed and said they could not be removed, as the city charter provided that all regularly appointed police in the annexed territory should be retained. The men indicated they would bring their situation to court. Inspector Cross said both the Rockaway Beach and Arverne stations would become substations to a new Far Rockaway Precinct.[85]

For over a month the men of the College Point police force waited anxiously for the answer regarding their status with the New York City Police Department. In early February they received the answer they feared – they were all summarily dismissed.[86]

Shortly after the consolidation went into effect on January 1, 1898, two New York Police sergeants appeared at Newton Town Hall and took charge of police operations in the town. The old town officials were instructed to keep performing their duties as usual until further instructions were received.[87] Shortly thereafter, the 77th Precinct was established in Newtown and in April, 1898 Captain Thomas J. Diamond was assigned as the commanding officer. Unlike the other Queens towns and villages, Newtown, which had recently changed its name to Elmhurst, had not hastily organized a police department prior to the consolidation, so the presence of the New York Police representatives caused little controversy.[88]

This was the first shield of the Police Department of the City of New York after it's consolidation in 1898.

HON. JOHN McCULLAGH

First Chief of Police of Greater New York

Big Bill Devery

Justice Garret J. Garretson

THE BATTLE FOR THEIR JOBS:

In August 1898 Ex-Captain Hickman left for a visit to Saratoga for his health. Before departing he confided to a friend that the lawyer representing the Whitestone police had informed him that the New York City Police Commissioners had agreed to reinstate the Whitestone village police and the Board of Estimate and Apportionment had provided funds to pay their salaries since January 1st. He said the former cops would be placed in the seventh grade at $800 a year. [89]

Notwithstanding Hickman's rumor, the Board of Police Commissioners had made it clear they did not want the members of the old village police forces included in the new police department of the City of Greater New York. Ultimately, the new City Charter that the commissioners hoped would protect them actually worked against them. The Charter provided that all members of a bona fide police department in Queens County on December 31, 1897 would be absorbed into the new police department of the Greater City. The Charter said nothing about how long someone was a policeman before December 31st. The question for the judge adjudicating these cases seemed to be whether or not the Queens lawmen were really police officers, not how long they were police officers.

The majority of the cases were heard by Justice Garret J. Garretson. Justice Garretson spent 21-years on the Supreme Court bench. Before becoming a judge, Garretson was the President of the Board of Education in Newtown for fifteen years and School Commissioner of Queens County for another three years. Throughout 1898 and beyond there were some mixed, and sometimes contradictory results to these cases.

The former policemen from the towns and villages of Queens wasted no time in filing numerous lawsuits requesting reinstatement to the New York City Police Department. The first case to get before Justice Garretson was Robert Rau, one of the policemen from the Village of Rockaway Beach at the time of consolidation. Through his attorney, Rau asked to be restored to the police force of New York, seventh grade, at a yearly salary of $800. Rau's papers showed that he was a duly appointed policeman of the Village of Rockaway Beach, and that he was legally holding that office on the 31st day of December 1897, and that by the Charter provisions he should be allowed to continue in office.

All the other deposed officers from Rockaway Beach and the rest of Queens knew the reality. Cases involving other officers from other villages were adjourned until the Rau case was decided. Their fates likely rested in the Rau decision.[90]

Approximately a month after receiving the case Justice Garretson rendered a decision ordering the board of police commissioners to reinstate Robert Rau and place him in the sixth grade. Counsel for New York City had argued that there had been no need for a police force to be established in Rockaway Beach, and therefore its establishment was evidence of intention to defraud the Greater City of New York. Justice Garretson rejected the City's argument on the grounds that it was not supported by any evidence.

Although the decision specifically dealt with Robert Rau, the popular belief was that it would affect all the other members of the former Rockaway Beach Village police force as well as most of the deposed policemen from the other villages and towns in Queens.

Justice Garretson only ordered Rau's reinstatement. He did not specify a date for his return. There was still anxiety running among the ex-Queens policemen due to an experience in Long Island City about a year earlier. In that case, nine members of the Long Island City Police Department who had been dismissed by Mayor Gleason obtained an order from the Supreme Court directing their return to duty. Gleason ignored the order and the nine men had not been returned to duty when Long Island City became part of the new Greater City of New York. What if the Board of Police Commissioners shrugged their collective shoulders and ignored Justice Garretson?[91]

While the details of Justice Garretson's decision were still being worked out, progress continued in the new city police department. On May 26th, Acting Chief of Police Devery was accompanied by many high-ranking members of the police department to join prominent political officials from Queens in Rockaway Beach on Henry Street for the laying of the cornerstone for the new Seventy-ninth sub-precinct.[92]

Wait a minute! What happened to Chief McCullagh? Although McCullagh had been a respected police leader, he was a Republican. The mayor had not forgotten about his marching orders from Tammany Hall to make William Devery Chief of Police. Very quietly, Captain Devery had been elevated to Deputy Chief, bypassing the rank of Inspector completely.

As dedicated as he was, Chief McCullagh's political affiliation doomed him from the start. Mayor Van Wyck exercised his executive privilege and removed the two Republican commissioners from office. In their place he named a more pliable Republican, Jacob Hess, and to guarantee no chance of a deadlocked vote he left the fourth commissionership vacant until such time as a new police chief was named. The reformed board quickly voted to retire McCullagh on a $3,000 annual pension and appoint William Devery the new Chief of Police. Tammany Hall had gotten its man.[93]

Even today, Big Bill Devery's name remains synonymous with corruption and graft. Devery grew so rich on the graft that he became part owner of the New York Highlanders baseball team, which later became the Yankees. New York's last Police Chief, before the position of Commissioner was recreated, Devery set a new low for police integrity and ethics, but he was also a beloved character. Reporters knew if they wanted a good quote, or Big Bill's acerbic opinions on the new mayors, the police department, or anything else, Devery would supply it. He was extremely colorful, funny and unfettered by common standards of decency. With no filter, Devery would say anything that came to his mind. The crusading journalist and author Lincoln Steffens summed up what many felt about Devery, "As a Chief of Police, he is a disgrace, but as a character, he is a work of art."

On Dec. 30, 1891, after 13 years on the force, Devery became a captain after paying $14,000. Put in charge of Eldridge Street station, the center of New York's red-light district, he famously told his men, "They tell me there's a lot of grafting going on in this precinct. They tell me that you fellows are the fiercest ever on graft. Now that's going to stop! If there's any grafting to be done, I'll do it. Leave it to me."

On Feb. 5, 1897, he was arrested and charged with bribery and extortion. Devery was convicted and dismissed from the force, but he appealed his conviction, and it was overturned. Reinstated to the force, Devery was amazingly promoted to Deputy Chief on Feb. 14, 1898, and then Chief of Police on June 30, 1898, despite an outcry from anti-corruption advocates.

As time passed, Devery was able to find a source of graft in the consolidation of New York's police forces. In 1898, shortly after the consolidation, Chief McCullagh standardized the uniform for the existing New York City police and the officers from the eighteen local police departments that were absorbed into the new Greater New York City Police Department. New uniform buttons, referred to as the "Consolidation" buttons, were part of the new uniform.

In 1901, Mayor Van Wyck appointed the NYPD's first solo Police Commissioner, Colonel Michael C. Murphy. Murphy was a former military man who served as the President of the New York City Board of Health. Whether Murphy was pre-disposed to graft or was influenced by the well-heeled Devery remains a mystery. Regardless, Murphy recognized the opportunity to utilize his position for his own financial benefit. Allegations were unofficially made that Murphy took a "cut" on all of the buttons purchased. Unlike Devery whose graft and corrupt practices brought him tens, if not hundreds, of thousands of dollars, Murphy made his money penny by penny.

On about June 11, 1901, Commissioner Murphy issued an order directing the 7,500 members of the uniformed force to purchase a new style of uniform button by July 1, 1901. The old buttons were made of brass, and the new of "Prince's Metal Oreide" and were double plated with 24 carat gold. The new buttons were patented one August 6, 1901. The Seal of the City of New York and the words "New York City Police" were on the face of the new buttons. The Consolidation buttons bore the city seal and had no words.

Why the change? Murphy stated he believed that when wearing the old buttons, police officers could not be identified as such and were mistaken for streetcar conductors. No examples of said confusion were offered.

Immediately, the members of the force were irate, not only because they were forced to pay for the buttons themselves, but because of the comparatively exorbitant cost (15 cents per button) compared to the existing buttons (7 cents each).

On January 24, 1902, Murphy's successor, Police Commissioner John C. Partridge, issued an order that dispensed with the Murphy Button and re-authorized the Consolidation button, which preceded that of Murphy's. In addition to the corrupt manner in which the Murphy button was adopted, they were below par on quality and design. Officers complained that the front and back pieces of the two-part buttons came apart easily and that a sharp shank on the rear damaged the uniform's cloth. Officers were not reimbursed for the cost of switching back to the Consolidation button and for those officers who held onto the old Consolidation buttons, there was no additional cost to the officers. More than 3,000 Murphy buttons on-hand by the department as well as those in possession of private tailors were returned to the manufacturer.

It turned out that the Board of Police Commissioners had not ignored Justice Garretson's decision to reinstate Robert Rau, they had decided to appeal the decision. On June 13th the Appellate Division of the Supreme Court affirmed the decision compelling the New York City Board of Police Commissioners to reinstate Robert Rau as a policeman in the New York City Police department.[94]

The men of the old College Point police force had also initiated their own legal action seeking reinstatement to the New York Police Department, and the case was also heard by Judge Garretson in the New York Supreme Court.[95]

On April 16th Justice Garrettson ordered the reinstatement of all eight members of the College Point Police force, including Captain Wohlfarth and Sergeant Williams.[96] The joy of the College Point men was tempered when a month passed, and the New York Board of Police Commissioners had taken no action on the judge's order to reinstate them. They went back to court and secured a peremptory writ of mandamus directing the Police Commissioners to restore the men to the force immediately and granting them back pay from January 1st.[97]

In June, the old College Point men were still not back on the job. In the meantime, the police station in College Point was moved out of Meyer's Store into larger quarters inside the Freygang Building.[98] Finally, in July, Captain Wohlfarth was summoned to Manhattan and advised that the Board of Police Commissioners desired to resolve the College Point situation. Wolhfarth was told that the entire College Point force would be reinstated immediately if Captain Wohlfarth and Sergeant Williams would relinquish the claim to their ranks and enter the New York Police Department as patrolmen.[99] Again, the College Point men found themselves back in court, and again, they were victorious.

The old college point policemen who were deposed shortly after the municipal consolidation were restored to duty. They were ordered to appear before Chief Devery and were promptly reinstated to their respective ranks and assigned duty in various parts of the city. Frederick Wohlfarth was assigned to duty as a captain in the Flushing precinct, and all the reinstated personnel received back pay from the time they were dismissed.[100]

On September 13th the Police Board restored thirteen policemen from the Borough of Queens appointed before consolidation, but whom the Board refused to recognize until ordered to do so by the Supreme Court. Thomas and Richard Hickman were among those reinstated – Denis Carll was not reinstated. Richard Hickman, however, was reinstated as a patrolman, not a captain. Hickman was assigned to patrol duties in Rockaway.[101]

1898 was many years away from the age of instant communication, but news still travelled, and very good or bad news found a way to travel quite quickly. Patrolman Richard Hickman was patrolling his beat in Rockaway when he learned that Louis Kreuscher and Frederick Wohlfarth had not only won their reinstatement cases, but they had been reinstated at the rank of captain. When Hickman went off duty, he hurried to his lawyer's office and bombarded him with an assortment of choice words. Hickman's counsel, John J. Gleason, wrote a letter to the Police Board, holding that Hickman was entitled to a captaincy and asking the board to give him that appointment. The Board replied that Hickman was reinstated as a member of the force by the court and that nothing was stated in the reinstatement about making him a captain. Gleason cited Kreuscher and Wohlfarth in his rebuttal, and all Hickman could do was return to his beat and wait.[102]

As the calendar changed to September there was optimism that the flood gates were slowly beginning to open when four members of the old Rockaway Beach police force and one member of the Arverne force were notified to report to New York Police headquarters for reinstatement processing. The joy and excitement of the five men involved as well as other ex-Queens policemen hoping for reinstatement was somewhat tempered by the fact that Robert Rau, who brought the original lawsuit, was not among those notified to report to headquarters. There was a collective sigh of relief several days later, however, when Rau finally did receive notice to report for reinstatement.[103]

Immediately after their ouster, Captain Hance and the men of his Flushing force retained a lawyer and obtained an assurance from Police Commissioner William E. Phillips that he would do everything in his power to have the Flushing Police reinstated. In the meantime, the citizens of Flushing started a fund to assist the former police in their legal battle for reinstatement.[104}

On March 24th the men of the former Flushing police force held their collective breaths as they waited to hear the decision in their first case requesting reinstatement to the New York City Police Department. The case to be decided was to be that of Henry Tompkins, the same Officer Tompkins who dodged the bullets of the gangs in the winter meadow, and the same Tompkins who was charged by Captain Hance with sleeping on duty. Even though this decision related only to Tompkins, all the members of the old Flushing police force knew that the decision for Tompkins would be the same for all of them. The Flushing men were elated when they learned that the Supreme Court issued an order directing the police commissioners to reinstate Henry Tompkins at once and to grant him back pay since the time of his removal.[105]

Despite the Supreme Court order in March, the heat of July still found the men of the old Flushing Village police still out in the cold. Representatives from New York City made an offer that they would drop all efforts of appeal and bring the Flushing men into the New York City Police Department immediately if all of the men, including Captain Hance, would agree to come into the department as patrolmen. Captain Hance said he did not want to stand in the way of his men being brought into the New York Department, so he signed an agreement that made him a patrolman in the New York City Police Department. Hance's loyalty to his men would come back to haunt him.[106]

The policemen who constituted the police force of Flushing before the consolidation act was passed were restored to duty by Chief Devery and performed duty in Rockaway in civilian clothes. Metropolitan Police badges were issued, and the men were fitted for uniforms.[107]

It took until September, but finally, the men of the old Richmond Hill village police force won their lawsuit for reinstatement to the New York Police Department. Not everyone was happy, however. Captain Baldwin was brought into the department as a patrolman – not a captain.[108]

Justice Garrett J. Garrettson handed down a decision denying the application for reinstatement of the police of Far Rockaway – William J. McVay, Herman Knebel, John H. Abrams, Charles A. Wheelwright, William G. Roberts, George Hemmert, John Fogarty, and Captain John Walsh.[109]

The question in the Hemmert case was the central issue in many of the other cases. Was Hemmert actually a policeman in the Arverne and Far Rockaway police forces

89

within the meaning of the New York Charter. The Charter was critical because it defined exactly who would be absorbed into the Greater New York Police Department when consolidation occurred on January 1, 1898. The relevant section of the charter read as follows:

The captain and each sergeant, roundsman and patrolman of the police force of the county of Richmond, or any town or village in that part of the County of Queens included in the City of New York, as hereby constituted, shall be members of the police force specified in section two hundred and seventy-six of this act.

Any patrolman of the police force of the village of Far Rockaway or Arverne by the Sea, who occupied that position at the time of consolidation became entitled to its benefits, in as much as the village was situated in that part of Queens County which was included by consolidation into the new City of New York, and the effect of the section of the Charter was to make such patrolmen members of the police force of the consolidated municipality. But was Hemmert a patrolman of the Arverne village police force? The New York State Supreme Court concluded he was not. Hemmert had not been paid a salary, nor did it appear that he ever received any compensation from the village except for $4.00. The judge concluded that for all intents and purposes, Hemmert was nothing more than a village constable, and it was not the intention of the legislation to transfer persons holding such positions, devoting only a portion of their time to their public duties and dependent upon fees for compensation, to the permanent police force of the Greater New York.[110]

Meanwhile, Patrolman Richard Hickman finally got his day in court. The issue was tried after much delay, in the Supreme Court before Justice Garretson, and resulted in a triumph for the deposed captain. The judge made an order reinstating Hickman as a captain of police for the City of New York. Hickman was elated, the document seeming all that was necessary to put him in the place to which he aspired and to which he felt that he was justly entitled.

A certified copy of the order was served on Commissioner York, but to the great surprise of Hickman and his counsel, York refused to recognize it. The order was amended making Hickman a "member" of the police force of the City of New York, but again, saying nothing about the rank of captain. This time, however, Hickman's lawyer, Gleason was relentless, and with the pressure of his persistence, his efforts were successful. Hickman was still engaged in patrolling Rockaway Beach as the police department considered whether or not to fight the decision. Corporation Counsel Whalen thought it best not to appeal the decision so Chief Devery assigned Hickman to the Mercer Street station house to be schooled in the duties of a captain.[111] No more resistance was offered and Hickman was made captain and assigned to duty in the Newtown precinct in July 1899.

In 1900 Denis Carll finally received his day in court when the New York State Supreme Court took up his case for appointment to the New York City Police Department. In recapping the facts of the case, the judge recognized that the Board of Trustees of the Village of Whitestone was entitled by the Village Charter to appoint a marshal or marshals not exceeding four, for the village, who would have and exercise all the powers of constables in the village. The judge also noted that the trustees had the authority to organize and maintain a competent police force.

The judge said that in February 1892 the Board of Trustees appointed Carll captain of police to act without pay, until a resolution of the board would be passed requiring active duty of him and at the same meeting appointed him a marshal. On April 4, 1892 a further resolution was passed giving Carll a salary of $40 a month beginning on May 1, 1892. The judge noted that Carll acted as captain of police for the one-man force, but that his actual rank was questionable.

Although the question of his prospective rank did not appear in his petition, Justice Garretson noted that Carll's claim to the rank of Captain appeared to be based solely on the ground that one night, I.J. Merritt, President of the Board, wishing to attract his attention, called out: "Say, Captain!" After that incident the word captain was always attached to Carll's name, and he considered Mr. Merritt's remarks as acknowledging his title.[112]

Justice Garretson further recapped that Carll constituted the entire police force until January 3, 1896, when the board declared the office vacant, and after Carll refused to accept the resolution as a dismissal from the office, another resolution was passed on March 2, 1896 reaffirming the January resolution and specifically discharging and removing him from the office of policeman and captain of police and declaring that no such office existed. In April 1897 Carll claimed that his discharge was illegal and brought an action against the village to recover salary claimed to be due him, in which action judgement was entered in favor of the village in June 1898.

Justice Garretson continued that in May 1899 Carll commenced a proceeding against the Board of Police Commissioners of the City of New York to compel them under the New York City Charter incorporating Whitestone into New York City, to recognize him as a police captain.

Justice Garretson ruled that the office of captain of police, being a creation of the board of trustees of the village, could exist only during its pleasure, that it was also by the express terms of the charter terminable by the board. The justice continued that at the time of Carll's affiliation with the village police force he was a marshal, which under the meaning of the Charter of the City of New York, would rank him only as a constable, making him ineligible for transfer to the New York City Police Department, even as patrolman. Justice Garretson went on to rule that it was evident that Carll was not entitled to the relief he sought. No such office existed as captain of police of the village, as creation was only at the trustees pleasure. So too, the tenure of the officers appointed by the board was terminable at their pleasure by express language of the village charter. Carll may have been captain of police, but he also constituted the entire force, so that the village authorities could not be said to have organized a competent police force as authorized by the village charter. Justice Garretson reiterated that as a marshal, Carll would only qualify as a village constable.[113]

The commissioners of the New York Police Department believed many of the towns and villages established police forces late in 1897 to provide patronage jobs as police officers to political friends once consolidation took place. They denied the absorption of most of the Queens County towns and village police forces into the new city department, but in most instances, they were defeated in legal appeals requiring most of the men from the old village and town forces to be brought into the Greater New York Police Department at the ranks they held. When it became clear that they were not going to be able to stop most of the local Queens lawmen from entering the New York City Police Department, the Board of Commissioners established a school of instruction in the Borough of Queens, under the command of Sergeant Michael Smith of the Central Office Squad. Those members of the department who were formerly members of the forces of the Borough of Queens were required to attend the school for the purpose of being instructed in their duties as members of the New York City Police Department. Excellent results were obtained from the drill instruction, as evidenced by the fine performance of the Queens men at the Police Parade on June 1, 1898.[114]

There were some exceptions to the reinstatements, however. Benjamin Ashmead was denied entry to the New York Police Department, and he lost his appeal for inclusion on the grounds that, like Denis Carll, all his years as a constable did not make him a member of a bona fide police force.[115] His failure to gain entry into the new city police department did not seem to bother Benjamin Ashmead. He remained at his position as Queens Court Officer for thirty years, eventually rising to the position of Captain of the Court Officers. Ashcraft died in 1920 at the age of 58.[116]

Thomas Baldwin continued fighting to recover his captain's rank. In November of 1899 the Appelate Division of the Supreme Court affirmed the decision to deny Baldwin the rank of captain.[117]

In January 1900, while dealing with another request for reinstatement, Bernard York, President of the Board of Police Commissioners cited the case of Baldwin, who was now a Jamaica patrolman. In his case the court decided that the Police Commissioners had the power to fix Baldwin's position and to assign him to any duty they saw fit.[118]

The Consolidation Button

The Murphy Button

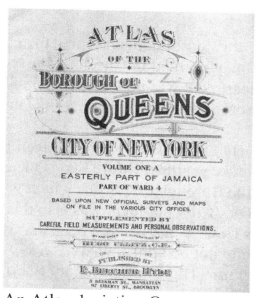

An Atlas depicting Queens as a Borough in
The City of New York

OWEN J. KAVANAGH.

Captain of Rockaway police arrested
In a Long Island City gambling raid.

AFTERMATH:

On face value, the consolidation seemed to simplify the law enforcement playing field in Queens. The New York City Police Department was now responsible for law enforcement in the Borough. But what about the Queens County Sheriff?

Law enforcement during 1898 was still laced with confusion. For the entire year there were two "Queens" entities. There was the Borough of Queens which was now a part of New York City, but there was also the remainder of Queens County that had not been part of the consolidation. It would not be until January 1, 1899 that Nassau County was born. The Queens County Sheriff, who had been responsible for policing Rockaway Beach before the organization of the Rockaway Beach police force, was still the primary law enforcement agency in the portion of Queens that had not been consolidated. In the Borough of Queens, the Sheriff's role evolved into primarily handling civil issues, but Sheriff William Baker still claimed the right to criminal law enforcement. He explained that the New York City Police Department would call upon the Sheriff's office when they had exhausted every means at their disposal to enforce the provisions and penalties of any law, and when they failed to do this for any reason, the Sheriff's Office would act immediately.[119]

The birth of Nassau County did not immediately end the confusion. The bill creating the new county allowed Queens officials to finish their terms, allowing Sheriff Baker to remain in office until January 1, 1901.[120]

When Captain Hickman was reinstated, he was sent to the Mercer Street Station for instruction under Captain Chapman. One day while on his way to the station house, an incident occurred which exemplified his tenacious quality as a police officer. His attention was attracted to a runaway team of horses as he was passing through Astor Place. The horses had made a plunge throwing out the occupant of the buggy and started off at a mad gallop. Hickman made a dash for the flying team as soon as they started and grabbed one of the horses by the head. He was unable to check the horses speed, however, and as a consequence he lost his footing, and continuing his hold, was dragged along by the infuriated team, in imminent danger of being trampled under their feet. After going about a hundred yards, the horse which the captain had grabbed slipped and fell, terminating the mad race. The man who had been thrown from the buggy escaped serious injury, and soon reached the spot where the run had finished. He thanked the captain for his brave act, but did not know to whom he was indebted, as Captain Hickman did not disclose his identity. The captain reached the station house pretty well bruised and battered, with a severe laceration of the arm. He received surgical treatment and went on his duties as usual.[121]

Things were looking up for Hickman. Not only had he regained his former captain's rank, but he also attended the fair in Whitestone to aid the building fund of the Immanuel Lutheran Church and won a 25-pound loaf of bread.[122]

With his captain's rank secured a rapid succession of transfers began. Hickman was transferred to Long Island City, but about four months later he was transferred again, this time to Flushing where he remained for only three months before being sent to Canarsie. From there, he was transferred to the 52nd Precinct in Brooklyn. While on vacation he was transferred back to Flushing, but before his vacation period expired the order was rescinded, and he continued command of the 52nd Precinct until June 1901 when he was placed in command of the 78th Precinct in Jamaica.[123]

In October of 1900 Captain Hickman was transferred to the Atlantic Avenue Station House. The precinct had been considered a "hoodoo" precinct on account of the mortality among the captains assigned there in the past and it may have been on this account that Hickman, who was only recently been sent to Atlantic Avenue from Canarsie, was so anxious to be sent away.[124]

Hickman was sent to Flushing and then to the Schenectady Avenue Precinct. He kept only an umbrella and a pair of rubbers in any station house where was in command, so that he was ready to move at a moment's notice, having been moved so many times since being reinstated to his rank.[125]

In July 1902 Hickman was again transferred, this time to Jamaica, switching places with Captain Wohlfarth. It was in this assignment that Hickman experienced his most serious police action.[126]

Suspicious men were seen eyeing the wire of the North Shore Railway and taking notice of the surrounding bushes and trees on New York Avenue near Locust Avenue. These materials were attractive targets for crooks prompting Captain Hickman to lay in wait for the wire thieves. On the third night of his stake out, Hickman was accompanied by Detectives Clarke and Clancy, and Patrolman Post. They waited for several hours but finally their patience was rewarded by the sight of two men silhouetted by the moonlight heading directly to the feed wire of the trolley line. The officers allowed them to make two cuts, and then they pounced. The crooks ran with Captain Hickman in pursuit of one of them.

"Halt, or I'll fire!" Hickman yelled.

As the Captain reached for his pistol it flew out of his hand and was lost in the thick bushes. His men had their guns out and a couple of bullets were pumped into a fleeing crook. The thief fell and was taken to the station house before being removed to the hospital, where he would spend two weeks before appearing in court. The wounded thief was named Salosky, a 35-year-old laborer from Brooklyn.[127]

In 1905 William McAdoo was the Commissioner of the New York City Police Department. One of McAdoo's projects was to weed out the old men on the force who were no longer physically capable of performing the job. Orders came out of Mulberry Street Police Headquarters on a regular basis directing members of the department to appear before the Board of Police Surgeons for examination. Captain Richard Hickman was one of these members.

Hickman received his examination and was shocked three months later to see his name among a list of 2-Inspectors, 10-captains, and 45-sergeants who were being retired because they were physically incapable of performing their duties.[128]

Once again, Captain Hickman found himself back in court suing for reinstatement and assignment to his former precinct in Jamaica. The 58-year-old produced medical certificates to show he was in perfect physical health. Hickman also claimed the police surgeon who signed the letter stating he was incapable of performing duty never examined him.[129]

On April 6, 1906 Supreme Court Justice Maddox granted a motion for Hickman's reinstatement.[130] And on April 13th Hickman was assigned to the 77th Precinct in Elmhurst, which was formerly called Newtown.[131]

On October 25, 1906 Captain Hickman had a homecoming when he was transferred to Whitestone.[132] Less than a year later Richard Hickman finally decided he had enough of police work and court battles. He voluntarily retired on half pay and devoted his life hereafter to enjoying himself and taking better care of his health. [133]

In 1908 another Hickman made the news. Captain Hickman's son, Thomas, had been a patrolman with the old Whitestone village police and had been retained after the consolidation when the litigation ordered the reinstatement of many of the village cops. The younger Hickman was accused of assaulting his sergeant, and in the process had his own left arm and two of his right fingers broken.

Sgt. Thomas Kenney said he found Hickman off his post, and when he reinstructed him on the violation Hickman tried to hit him with his club. The sergeant said Hickman sustained his injuries when he simply defended himself. Hickman was locked up and held on $500 bail. Later, Captain Leary, the precinct commanding officer, had Hickman paroled and he took him to his home and put him to bed in a surgeon's care.[134] The 42-year-old Hickman was married, lived in Whitestone, and had been on the force for seven years. He pled not guilty, claiming that Kenny hit him with his stick causing a severe laceration to his scalp.[135] On October 18th, 1908, Hickman was arraigned in the Flushing Court before Magistrate Connolly. The magistrate dropped the charges stating that he had been informed that Police Commissioner Bingham was handling the case internally.[136]

Captain Richard T. Hickman died at 2 AM on November 4, 1908, in his home from stomach troubles.[137] I could not find how the Police Commissioner adjudicated the case against Thomas Hickman, but apparently, he was not dismissed from the police department. On November 12th, 1908, Hickman was transferred from the Whitestone precinct to the 275th Precinct in Long Island City.[138]

Captain Hickman may have been dead, but that didn't mean he still wasn't in the news. On August 26th, 1910, Charles Mickel, a 50-year-old shoemaker from Jamaica was arrested after the police received complaints from a dozen residents of Willow Street. It seemed that Mickel was annoying these people by ringing their doorbells and acting in a peculiar manner. What was peculiar about what he was doing? The shoemaker said that Captain Hickman, who was formerly assigned to the Jamaica station house, had sent him to find a pair of his shoes.[139]

Mickel told the people who answered their doors that Hickman had directed him to repair the shoes once they were found. When Patrolman Leonard Quinn arrived on the scene, it didn't make much of an impression with Mickel when the officer told him Captain Hickman had been dead for two years. Mickel shrugged and insisted he had talked to the captain and had his orders to find the shoes. Patrolman Quinn utilized a bit of psychology and told Mickel that since the shoes had a police connection they should proceed to the precinct and search the station house. Mickle agreed and once at the precinct he was taken into custody and taken for observation to a Brooklyn Hospital.[140]

The saga of Denis Carll had not been completed. The deposed, self-proclaimed captain of the Whitestone police force had been appointed truant officer for the schools at Little Neck, Bayside, Queens, and Black Stump. The salary was $840 a year with traveling expenses. [141]

On June 5, 1900, Carll was removed from the position by Superintendent of Schools Edward Stevens on the ground that Carll's work was unsatisfactory. While still waiting for the resolution of his suit to compel the police board to recognize him as a captain of police, Carll sued the Board of Education for reinstatement as truant officer.

In October, Justice Josiah T. Marean in Supreme Court denied a motion for a writ of mandamus to compel the School Board of the Borough of Queens to reinstate Denis Carll as an attendance officer.[142]

In 1915 Denis Carll was honored for 40 years of service with the Whitestone Fire Department making him the senior man in the department.[143] Denis Carll died in Whitestone in January of 1920.[144]

After being assigned to the Flushing precinct after his reinstatement, Captain Frederick Wolhfarth was transferred to the Atlantic Avenue station house in Brooklyn because of his failure to suppress burglaries within the Flushing precinct. For the better part of the year Wohlfarth had been in command the burglars had their own way. No less than a hundred homes were entered during a six-month period with no arrests made. Things went from bad to worse until it got so that people were held up on the highway in broad daylight and made to give up their valuables. Hold-ups that would reflect credit upon an Oklahoma outlaw were perpetrated in Flushing and the public was thrown into a state of terror. At last Chief Devery decided to take a hand in the matter and make a change. Wohlfarth's replacement, Captain Richard Hickman, was well-known in Flushing and he brought a great deal of confidence in his ability to solve the problem.

Wohfarth's backers said the captain was receiving a raw deal because all the burglaries were being committed by the residents of Mrs. Ballington Booth's Hope Hall, a home for about a hundred ex-convicts in Flushing. In assuming command, Hickman said that if the colony of ex-convicts was responsible for the crime spree, he would arrest everyone in the residence if necessary.[145]

Captain Wohlfarth enjoyed success in command of the Atlantic Avenue Precinct in a peculiar manner. He was the first precinct commander to break the so-called "hoodoo" or spell which seemed to surround every captain assigned to the precinct. Somehow, no commander ever remained at the precinct for a long period of time. Death, transfer, or resignation caused the precinct to be known as the "hoodoo" of the borough. It was even said that the station house was haunted, and more than one captain refused to sleep there overnight. But Captain Wohlfarth did not believe in "hoodoo" or haunted houses with a tenure at the precinct of over three years.

Wohlfarth was born in College Point and became a policeman in Far Rockaway in 1886. One year later he became a sergeant during the regime of Sheriff Goldner and held that post for two years. He then took charge of the police on the Long Island Railroad on the run from Long Island City to Far Rockaway and subsequently became a railroad detective. He resigned from that post to become captain of the marshals in College Point and when in 1897 a police force was organized, he became captain.[146] Wohlfarth was forced to retire in 1925 and died in 1948 at the age of 85.

What about William Methven, who had been unceremoniously dumped as captain of the Rockaway Beach police force shortly before the consolidation? He wasn't considered for absorption into the New York City Police Department, but he didn't care. When Sheriff William Baker took office in January 1898 he kept Methven on as deputy sheriff, placing him in charge of the various festivals in Queens County and Camp Black. Camp Black was located in Garden City at the site of what is now called Mitchell Field. From April to September of 1898 Camp Black was a mustering-in location for Army troops before they were shipped out to fight in the Spanish-American War. The presence of the soldiers brought all manner of entrepreneurs, some legal and some illegal to the vicinity of the camp. Methven set up a headquarters tent at the camp and along with a contingent of deputies kept a close eye on the people and businesses springing up around the camp. Methven was praised for the job he performed at Camp Black, and when the camp closed in September of 1898, he returned to his normal duties in the Queens County Sheriff's Office. In December 1898 Sheriff Baker appointed Methven as his Undersheriff.[147]

In January of 1900 it was announced that Methven would be the Republican candidate for Sheriff in the election later in the year. William Methven's career was proceeding as well as he could have hoped until that afternoon in April of 1900 while he worked in his office inside the courthouse in Long Island City. At some point, Methven took a break from his paperwork and leaned back in his swivel chair to stretch. Unfortunately, he leaned back a little too far and the chair flipped backwards causing Methven to fall out of the chair and strike his head on a steam radiator. The wound was stitched up and Methven was transported to his Flushing home. After a few days it was found that instead of healing, the wound had festered and eryslpelas, a bacterial skin infection, had set in. On May 1st the wound was examined, and it was found that the bone had decayed. Surgery was performed to attempt to correct the problem, but Methven died shortly after the surgery. He was 49-years old.[148]

Charles Hance was tired. The former captain of the Flushing village police force, who had shown such loyalty to his men by signing an agreement to be reinstated as a patrolman so that his men would not have their reinstatements delayed, was 68-years old. Patrolling his beat in Far Rockaway had worn him down physically and in 1904 Patrolman Hance decided that he deserved a permanent vacation and filed for retirement from the New York City Police Department. [149] Charles hance died in 1921 at the age of 85.[150]

Rockaway's famous amusement park, Rockaway Playland, was built in 1901 and quickly became a major attraction for people around the region. With its growing popularity, concern over swimming etiquette became a problem and early in 1904, the Captain Louis Kreuscher added to the history of Rockaway and the amusement park by issuing rules for those using the beach, censoring the bathing suits to be worn, where photographs could be taken, and specifying that women in bathing suits were not allowed to leave the beachfront.

The New York City Police Department has a long and storied history filled with colorful characters, many heroes and a few villains. The men from Queens who kept the county safe before it was a Borough in the city, and who had to fight tooth and nail for their jobs and ranks after consolidation don't have monuments and awards to commemorate their service to the city. But Richard Hickman, Denis Carll, Charles Hance, Frederick Wohlfarth, Louis Kreuscher, and especially Henry Wendelsporf, who made the ultimate sacrifice in the line of duty, are an integral of the NYPD's rich legacy.

circa 1908

282nd Precinct covering Woodhaven, Glendale, and Ozone Park

The old 110th Precinct in Elmhurst when it was the 60th Pct. In 1907

74th sub-precinct -opened in 1899 it was on the site of what is now LaGuardia Airport

Old 85ᵗʰ Precinct – the old Meyers Mansion in Glendale opened in 1906

Postcard depicting the 274ᵗʰ Precinct in Astoria in 1908. It would eventually become the 114ᵗʰ Precinct

The old 65th Precinct in Flushing that would become the 109th Precinct

The Remonstrance was signed at a house on the site of the former State Armory, now the headquarters of the NYPD's Queens North Task Force and Strategic Response group 4

Bibliography

1. William, Keith, HOW QUEENS BECAME NEW YORK CITY'S LARGEST BOROUGH, 10/20/2015

2. Flushing village incorporation 1837 – charters by-laws and ordinances of the Village of Flushing

3. LONG ISLAND ITEMS, The Brooklyn Daily Eagle, 2/1/1870, p3

4. A CONSTABLE CONVICTED, The Brooklyn Daily Eagle, 2/4/1870, p3

5. UNTITLES, The Corrector, 12/24/1881, p2

6. BEATEN BY TWO GIRLS, The Evening Post, 7/2/1892, p10

7. STILL WEARS HIS UNIFORM, The Brooklyn Daily eagle, 1/16/1896, p7

8. NO SALARY FOR POLICE CAPTAIN, The Brooklyn Daily Eagle, 2/5/1896, p5

9. WHITESTONE'S POLICE FORCE, The Brooklyn Daily Eagle, 3/17/1896, p5

10. O'CONNOR AGAIN ACCUSED, Brooklyn Times Union, 10/22/1896, p6

11. TONY TO SUFFER ALONE, Times Union, 12/18/1896, p9

12. ONE WOMANS CURIOSITY, The Standard Union, 10/22/1895, p2

13. LUGAR-WENDELSTORF, Times Union, 2/11/1897, p7

14. FIRST ARREST AT WHITESTONE, The Brooklyn Daily Eagle, 8/7/1896, p5

15. THREATENED LYNCHING, Times Union, 6/25/1897, p7

16. MOB THREATENS NEGROES, The Sun, 6/25/1897, p3

17. NORFLEET'S TRIAL, Times Union, 6/29/1897, p7

18. NORFLEETS'S SENTENCED, The Standard Union, 1/22/1898, p12

19. SOLD FOR UNPAID TAXES, The Brooklyn Daily Eagle, 11/16/1897, p5

20. FOR MRS. WENDELSTORF, Times Union, 5/6/1898, p8

21. WHITESTONE POLICE, The Brooklyn Daily eagle, 12/1/1897, p11

22. WHITESTONE'S POLICE FORCE, The Brooklyn Daily Eagle, 12/16/1897, p5

23. COLLEGE POINT POLICE, Brooklyn Times Union, 4/11/1888, p1

24. FLUSHING, Times Union, 12/12/1888, p5

25. AMBROSE MARTIN, Times Union, 1/29/1907, p8

26. COLLEGE POINT POLICE, Times Union, 1/11/1895, p3

27. MARTIN'S FRIENDS AT WORK, Times Union, 1/17/1895, p3

28. BURGLARS ARE COMING, Brooklyn Times Union, 2/15/1897, p7

29. COLLEGE POINT'S POLICE, The Brooklyn Daily Eagle, 5/22/1897, p5

30. COLLEGE POINT POLICE FORCE, Brooklyn Times Union, 6/18/1897, p7

31. COLLEGE POINT POLICE, Brooklyn Times Union, 7/1/97, p6

32. FLUSHING POLICE ARRANGEMENTS, The Brooklyn Daily Eagle, 2/25/1871, p3

33. CAPTAIN CHARLES HANCE, The Brooklyn Daily eagle, 9/4/1898, p13

34. THE FLUSHING POLICE, Times Union, 11/21/1887, p1

35. NOT POLICEMEN ENOUGH, The Times Union, 12/10/1887, p1

36. WAS THE OFFICER ASLEEP, The Times Union, 7/20/1897, p7

37. FLUSHING POLICE FORCE, Times Union, 12/9/1897, p6

38. A CONSTABLE'S BARN NOT A GOOD PLACE FOR STOLEN HARNESS, The Times Union, 4/15/1889, p5

39. UNTITLED, The Brooklyn Daily Eagle, 6/13/1897, p12

40. MR. STANFORDS'S ACTION, Times Union, 6/14/1897, p7

41. A PETITION TO THE BOARD, Times Union, 7/7/1897, p6

42. POLICE FORCE FOR JAMAICA TOWN, Times Union, 11/10/1897, p7

43. CHARGES AGAINST A POLICE CAPTAIN, The Brooklyn Daily Eagle, 12/17/1895, p7

58. RECEPTION TO CAPTAIN METHVEN, The Brooklyn Daily Eagle, 8/18/1897, p5

59. FOR ROCKAWAY BEACH POLICE, The Standard Union, 10/30/1897, p6

60. ROCKAWAY BEACH POLICE, Times Union, 11/19/1897, p6

61. UNTITLED, The Standard Union, 9/3/1889, p4

62. RIOTERS ARRAIGNED, The Standard Union, 7/7/1896, p5

63. KILLED A STOLEN COW, The Brooklyn Daily Eagle, 11/13/1893, p2

64. UNTITLED, The Brooklyn Daily Eagle, 10/25/1893, p2

65. UNTITLED, Brooklyn Daily Eagle, 1/2/1898, p10

66. UNTITLED, The Brooklyn Daily Eagle, 1/27/1898, p13

67. A LITTLE TO PREVIOUS, The Brooklyn Daily Eagle, 12/22/1897, p4

68. UNTITLED, The Brooklyn Daily Eagle, 1/3/1898, p2

69. NEW YOR OFFICIALS TAKE A PRELIMINARY LOOK AT FLUSHING, COLLEGE POINT AND WHITESTONE, The Brooklyn Daily Eagle, 12/28/1897, p5

70. NEW POLICEMEN IN CHARGE OF FLUSHING COLLEGE POINT, The Brooklyn Daily Eagle, 1/2/1898, p4

71. UNTITLED, The Brooklyn Daily Eagle, 1/3/1898, p3

87. UNTITLED, The Brooklyn Daily Eagle, 1/3/1898, p3

88. CAPTAIN DIAMOND IN CHARGE, The Brooklyn Citizen, 4/17/1898, p9

89. WILL SUE FOR RANK, Brooklyn Times Union, 8/12/1898, p8

90. A TEST POLICE CASE, The Brooklyn Daily Eagle, 3/6/1898, p10

91. UNTITLED, Times Union, 4/4/1898, p2

92. CORNER STONE LAYING, Times Union, 5/24/1898, p9

93. Whalen and Doorey, The Birth of the NYPD, 1998

94. RAU TO BE REINSTATED, The Standard Union, 6/14/1898, p8

95. SEEKING REINSTATEMENT, Brooklyn Times Union, 3/4/1898, p7

96. UNTITLED, Brooklyn Daily Eagle, 4/17/1898, p34

97. THECOURT DIRECTS THAT THEY BE PAID FROM JANUARY 1, The Times Union, 5/5/1898, p9

98. QUEENS BOROUGH NOTES, The Brooklyn Daily Eagle, 6/20/1898, p4

99. UNTITLED, Times Union, 7/8/1898, p8

100. COLLEGE POINT POLICE WIN, The Brooklyn Daily Eagle, 10/27/1898, p12

101. POLICEMEN REINSTATED, The Standard Union, 9/14/1898, p6

102.   WANTS TO BE A CAPTAIN, The Brooklyn Daily Eagle, 11/14/1898, p12

103.   BACK ON THE FORCE, Times Union, 9/12/1898, p7

104.   FLUSHING POLICEMEN HOPEFUL, The Brooklyn Daily Eagle, 2/4/1898, p10

105.   FLUSHING POLICE REINSTATED, The Brooklyn Daily Eagle, 3/24/1898, p5

106.   CAPTAIN HANCE AND OTHER OFFICERS WILLING TO SACRIFICE RANK FOR THE SAKE OF THEIR FELLOWS, Times Union, 7/8/1898, p8

107.   FLUSHING POLICE REINSTATED, Times Union, 9/9/1898, p7

108.   POLICEMEN REINSTATED, The Standard Union, 9/14/1898, p6

109.   NOT POLICEMEN NOW, The Brooklyn Citizen, 1/4/1899, p9

110.   NEW YORK SUPPLEMENT 1899 p401

111.   CAPTAIN HICKMAN REINSTATED, The Brooklyn Daily Eagle, 6/19/1899, p2

112.   DUBBED CAPTAIN BY MERRITT, The Brooklyn Daily Eagle, 2/8/1900, p7

113.   PEOPLE EX REL CARLL V. YORK, Second Department, July Term, 1900, p429

114.   1899 New York City Police Department Annual Report, p21-22

Made in United States
North Haven, CT
10 February 2023

32329724R00068